PENGUIN BOOKS

WEDIQUETTE

Yetta Fisher Gruen worked for eighteen years for *The Washington Post* at the Bridal Desk. The Bridal page, which appears each Wednesday in the Style section and has a large reader interest, prompted the public to telephone questions to her about wedding etiquette. Fascinated by the types of queries, Mrs. Gruen realized that some questions were a lot more serious or deeper than they appeared to be on the surface and that a book was needed on the subject. Her expertise comes from research, from talking to people about their experiences, and from her instinct about voices on the telephone. Born and educated in England, Mrs. Gruen lives in Bethesda, Maryland. She has two sons, a daughter-in-law, and two grandsons.

Wediquette

THE ANSWERS TO ALL YOUR

WEDDING ETIQUETTE QUESTIONS

Yetta Fisher Gruen

PENGUIN BOOKS

PENGUIN BOOKS
Published by the Penguin Group
Penguin Books USA Inc., 375 Hudson Street,
New York, New York 10014, U.S.A.
Penguin Books Ltd, 27 Wrights Lane,
London W8 5TZ, England
Penguin Books Australia Ltd, Ringwood,
Victoria, Australia
Penguin Books Canada Ltd, 10 Alcorn Avenue,
Toronto, Ontario, Canada M4V 3B2
Penguin Books (N.Z.) Ltd, 182–190 Wairau Road,
Auckland 10, New Zealand

Penguin Books Ltd, Registered Offices:
Harmondsworth, Middlesex, England

Your Wedding was first published in Penguin Books 1986
This revised and updated edition titled Wediquette
published in Penguin Books 1995

1 3 5 7 9 10 8 6 4 2

LIBRARY OF CONGRESS CATALOGING IN PUBLICATION DATA
Gruen, Yetta Fisher.
Wediquette : the answers to all your wedding etiquette questions /
Yetta Fisher Gruen.
p. cm.
Includes index.
ISBN 0 14 02.4139 6
1. Wedding etiquette. I. Title.
BJ2051.G78 1995
395'.22—dc20   94-34803

Printed in the United States of America
Set in Adobe Stempel Schneidler
Designed by Ann Gold

TO MY LATE HUSBAND, BERTRAM

Author's Note

There is a French saying: "The more things change, the more they stay the same." It holds true for wedding protocol as well as etiquette—the trend is back to the traditional.

Questions on wedding etiquette began to increase over my eighteen years at the Bridal Desk of *The Washington Post*. Then, as now, my research from books written in the 1780s to the present has been of immeasurable help. What a comfort to be able to read Amy Vanderbilt, Emily Post, and Oretha D. Swartz along with numerous magazines and wedding advice books, and to find most in agreement. I am glad to have had these sources to draw on and adapt to the particular questions, not only from those planning a wedding but from those going to a wedding, as well as service such as musicians, caterers, and photographers.

Acknowledgments

To me it is important to first mention my late husband, Bertram, who throughout our marriage gave me his confidence in my ability to write, and for his help in the extensive research and his patience in reading the original manuscript of *Wediquette* so many times; my son Mark Howard Gruen, my computer guru and early editor, who gave me the input I needed in his specialty—music; my son Dr. Richard Alan Gruen—a physician and history buff—whose suggestions were invaluable; his wife, Ruth Jakubowski, for her loving support; and to my grandsons, Benjamin and Kenneth, who are a constant joy.

I also wish to thank Kathryn Court, editor in chief; my devoted and patient editors, Nicole Guisto and Leslie Hulse, at Penguin USA; and Mr. Ronald Goldfarb, Washington, D.C., lawyer and literary agent.

How does one value friendship and what does one say in appreciation? I am also grateful to Scotte Manns, former director of advertising at *The Washington Post*, for her encouragement and friendship over the years; to Elsie Selman, for her interest and suggestions; and to other friends, whose support was beyond the call of duty and common sense.

Thanks also go to Richard Harwood, former deputy managing editor at *The Washington Post* for accepting my first short stories to be published, which appeared in *The Washington Post* magazine section; to Dr. Mahinder Tak, a gracious lady who led me through the Hindu wedding, and also Mrs. Sumitra

Singh, librarian at the Embassy of India; Major Steven R. Rich, chaplain at Bolling Air Force Base in Washington, D.C., who was so generous with his time and his knowledge of military wedding ceremonies; to Ms. Susan Mannina, director of administration of the Church of St. Andrews, Lutheran, in Silver Spring, Maryland; to Mr. Frank Massey of the Baltimore Yearly Meeting of the Religious Society of Friends; to Beverly Campbell of the Church of Jesus Christ of Latter-Day Saints, Mormon; to Mrs. Shirley Chilson, the North American Division of the Seventh-Day Adventist Church; to the Reverend Father Hughes, former associate pastor of St. Mary's Catholic Church in Rockville, Maryland; to Father John of St. Sophia Greek Orthodox Cathedral in Washington, D.C.; to Rabbi Tzvi H. Porath, rabbi emeritus of Ohr Kodesh Congregation, Conservative, in Chevy Chase, Maryland; and to Rabbi Emeritus Joshua Haberman of the Washington Hebrew Congregation, Reform, in Washington, D.C.

Among other countless books, source material was found in the *Encyclopaedia Britannica* and in the Library of Congress (where I studied while trying not to spend most of my time admiring its magnificent architecture). I also wish to acknowledge a debt of gratitude to all those who asked me all those questions for all those years.

Contents

Introduction

"Feelings, feelings, nothing but feelings" can turn into questions, questions, nothing but questions when planning a wedding. Knowing how traditions are passed from one generation to another is one thing; puzzling out the intricacies of bringing together two families who have nothing in common except that their children are in love often requires a great deal of understanding on both sides, even though there is no objection to the match.

Some questions combine those of protocol and of human relationships; other queries concern straightforward wedding etiquette. To navigate the maze successfully, one must separate protocol and etiquette from tangled family situations. The answers can ensure a happy wedding day as well as a strong family foundation on both sides.

Wediquette evolved from the many questions asked of me from the inception of *The Washington Post*'s Bridal Desk. It became apparent that the public needed a book that takes an in-depth look at the whole wedding process from all sides: the bride's point of view, the bridegroom's, both of their families', the guests', and the services'. Because wedding etiquette is not set in concrete and these "rules" change as society evolves, discussing questions can help the reader to make decisions to suit his or her particular needs.

Knowing what is generally done helps us make choices based on knowledge rather than guesswork. Knowing what

others have experienced helps us understand the process of decision making. After all, how many weddings does a family
sponsor in a lifetime? How many functions larger than a dinner
or cocktail party has any of us planned, to say nothing of the
emotional aspect—actions, reactions, and counteractions
within families?

What is relatively easy is the gathering of the services, such
as those of a caterer, photographer, and engraver, needed for a
successful event. What is more difficult is the complexity of
human relations, which can be hard to fathom. Even families
who have known each other for years can become sensitive
about decisions regarding their children's marriage. For example, the bride's family may be waiting for his parents to offer
to pay part of the wedding expenses; but the bridegroom's parents do not see it that way. Perhaps the expenses are being
split down the middle, giving both sides the chance to have an
equal say.

There are times when I am asked a question and I sense
there is more to the story than the query indicates. I cite the
basic etiquette question below—though it is used elsewhere in
this book in a simpler context—as an example of etiquette's
more complicated aspects:

*Q: Is it obligatory to attend a church ceremony when invited only to
the church and not to the wedding reception?*

Accepting or declining an invitation to attend any event is
up to the individual. Who asks if he *has* to go to any function?
The phrasing of this query suggested to me that it was a surface
one. An invitation to the church ceremony carries no pressure;
not even a reply is expected. The answer to that question is
found in various wedding books. But the second layer revealed
a dilemma. Suppose an employer asks the question? The bridegroom has worked for him for the past fifteen years, and ap-

parently he finds the young man an asset. Mr. and Mrs. Employer have even entertained the young couple in their home. Yet when the invitation arrived they were surprised to find they were invited only to the ceremony. They were perplexed and really did not want to attend.

Careful thought should have gone into the decision to extend a limited invitation to Mr. and Mrs. Employer. Though it sometimes cannot be helped, I have uncomfortable feelings about this situation that I discuss elsewhere in this book. What bothers me most is that the bridegroom did not question a decision that would more than likely hurt his relationship with his employer. Not only does the young man make a living working for that firm but perhaps his employer was keeping him in mind for promotion. When he was asked about it, the bridegroom responded, "I don't have anything to do with it. They're arranging the whole thing." By disclaiming any involvement, he sets a bad precedent, which does not augur well for the health of his relationship with his wife. What is he saying? She'll make the mistakes in this family; he will have nothing to do with the decision making, so it will be her fault if plans go awry! It was *his* employer and wife who were put in an awkward position. Someone should have pointed out to the young man that inaction is an action in itself and that silence is taken as acquiescence.

There must have been another alternative. Perhaps the reception site was too small to accommodate the guest list, which suggests poor planning. I doubt the reason given to me would have mollified anyone: That is, the bride, in order to reap many gifts, invited a church full of guests but only the bridal party and the couple's family to the reception.

The way decisions are made is the key to good relationships. Some parents are take-charge types; they evaluate what they can or cannot do and go on from that point. Others agonize that they simply are not meeting the needs or expectations of others. They feel the happiness of their child hinges on the upcoming events and cannot forget that they are dealing with strangers—their child's future in-laws.

As for the wedding itself, when one is considering a change in a traditional wedding, the determining factors should be: Does the change have to do with religious rites? If it does, permission has to be obtained from the officiant. The next question is: Will the change offend? Is the procedure just a mite different from the norm, and is it in good taste?

However, there is greater leeway when arranging the other elements; and though people are going back to more traditional weddings, there are elements that will not change.

At one time, a divorcée's remarriage was conservative, and many still are. But others, some think, overdo the wedding bit. In the past, the feelings conveyed by some of the dos and don'ts of wedding etiquette were unfair to widows and divorcees—a leftover attitude of history toward such women. In Western society the attitude mainly took the form of mild disdain toward divorcées, whereas widows were expected to behave quietly (and preferably not be there?). In some sects in India, for example, a widow was expected to throw herself on her deceased husband's funeral pyre.

What about the first-time bridegroom? He was told that he could not have a wedding celebrating his only marriage because his bride had been previously married. But that is also changing.

To me these changes are minor. The major, time-honored conventions of weddings remain the same. Most cultures recognize that marriage is the most important step a man and a woman can take and that society benefits from the solid structure that the union brings: an umbrella of protection for children and continuity with the past. Nothing I have read convinces me that there has been a successful substitute.

Whether the marriage is conducted by a justice of the peace or by a person of the cloth, the components are the same—the hopeful promises, the company in attendance, and the feting that follows. The world may not celebrate the event, but the immediate circle of the bride and bridegroom does. From that group comes a sense of security that most couples experience when they decide to marry.

Engagement

The Promise

*T*he engagement period is a special time. Everything seems so right. The impermanence of dating and the uncertainty that one or the other may have felt before making the commitment have been overcome. The engaged couple feel the excitement and see their friends' and families' happiness when they learn the news. The prospect of exchanging vows still generates a special kind of excitement, even if the couple has been living together.

This delicate time is a balance of pleasure and pressure. Family, friends, and acquaintances can be nonchalant about the couple while they are dating but when the words "we're going to be married" are announced, everyone takes his or her place in the formalities—like chess pieces at the start of the game.

Though people do not always marry their first love, their choices are their own and freely made, which was not so in the past in Europe. In fact, marriages are still arranged in some Eastern cultures.

In 1986, when this book was first printed, I quoted a charming Indian woman, a professor at one of our Ivy League universities: "Our system of marrying off our children works," she said at that time. "In America the focus is on the individual. In my country, the whole family is of central importance to us as well as the *sect* from which the family stems—all are reliant one on the other. Besides, love comes later."

I recently had an interesting conversation with an East Indian mother of three daughters, the eldest of whom is a college student. She has lived with her Indian husband in America for most of her married life.

"All over India the attitude is broadening about marriage within the *sects*," she told me. "Especially in the metropolises, their main concern is that the bride and bridegroom are Hindu. My daughters understand that the choice of a husband is still up to my husband and me."

"What," I asked, "if your daughter meets a young Indian man at college."

"If we are impressed with him," she answered, "and the family is acceptable, my husband and I would approve."

"Does love come later?" I asked.

"Yes" was the emphatic response.

However, while most modern East Indian men and women feel that parental choice works, there are some recent signs of changes in attitude toward marrying in the same sect or religion—mainly, of course, those living in Western countries. It is understandable because people of different backgrounds meet at universities and in workplaces, where culture meet.

Here, in the United States, we hope romantic love deepens with maturity.

From the moment the betrothal is announced, the engaged couple start building their future. Now understanding of each other truly begins. Not only do they plan the wedding, but they also have to decide where they will live and how they wish to spend their money. If both are established in their chosen professions and own homes, does one rent out and live in the other's house? Do they sell? Will it be necessary to draw up a premarital contract if either or both have children from a previous marriage?

A couple in their twenties, just starting out, have to select living quarters, decide how they will support themselves, and learn how to manage their incomes. The type of wedding, however, is generally a decision based on what parents can afford.

We do not realize that we have mixed marriages in America, not just on racial or religious grounds but in the cultural sense. For example, Catholics may marry Catholics but the ethnicity can be different: a person of Italian descent might marry someone from an Irish, Polish, Spanish, or French background. An American and an Asian or an Arab might be surprised to the point of culture shock at the extent to which they have to adjust, not only to each other's foibles—as do most couples—but to each other's mores. It is wise to read about your fiancé(e)'s culture. A good deal is revealed during the courtship and the planning stages of the wedding.

Now the chess pieces are beginning to move. . . .

When telephoning your grandparents, you will hear their delighted responses to your news, which will be repeated by other close friends and members of both your families. You and your parents will be busy writing notes to close friends and they, in turn, pass on the news to others.

Before the bride's mother calls the newspaper to arrange for an announcement, she waits for the young man's mother to get in touch with her. But suppose nothing happens? Her daughter assures her that all is well. Her mother waits, since everyone knows that the bridegroom's mother contacts the bride's family to express her pleasure over the turn of events. After a while, the bride's mother telephones and finds a thrilled future mother-in-law on the other end of the line saying how pleased she and her husband are and what a lovely daughter they have. Then the bride's mother suggests they all meet at her house next Friday. Now both families can think about future plans.

Could it be that the bridegroom's mother just was not sure how to proceed? That the difficulty was not a lack of warmth but merely shyness? Or it might have seemed natural to her that she would hear from the bride's mother since it is customary for the bride's parents to handle all the arrangements. Suppose, however, the mother of the bride decided that it was not her place to call her future son-in-law's parents—never mind the state of his mother's psyche. That could be the beginning of a precarious relationship. Being socially correct is not always the right thing.

Follow the same protocol if the future bride's or the bridegroom's parents are divorced. It is the parent with whom the
young person lives who is contacted first. If the young person
lives with neither parent, then the mother is invited first and
the father later, or they might be invited together if the situation is stable.

Q: *My husband is hurt. A daughter from his first marriage has become engaged to a fine young man whom we've met many times. His
family and the bride's mother have gotten together. Because the future
groom's people haven't made a move to contact us, I've debated
whether to say something to my stepdaughter. What do you think?*

Tell your stepdaughter that you are telephoning her fiancé's
parents to extend a dinner invitation, which is possibly what
they were expecting. She and her fiancé will be pleased, as will
his parents. The relationship the bridal couple has with her
mother shouldn't prevent the loving one you and your husband
have established.

The Engagement Party

The engagement party is generally hosted by the bride's parents, but anyone may offer to do it. It is a great way for both
sides to meet extended families. If the bridegroom's people live
out of town, they might give a separate welcoming celebration
of their own. If possible, the bride's family is included.

Ladies and Gentlemen, some people have told me that they
first met their child's in-laws at the wedding. It might be difficult to arrange, but, on general principles, parents of the betrothed couple should meet before the wedding day, even if
one set of parents has to travel to do so.

Entertaining Future In-laws

Future in-laws entertain one another in various ways. Sometimes it is a large gathering at a country club or perhaps an informal get-together at home that gives the parents a chance to talk about wedding plans.

Introductions to friends and family may take place in a more casual manner on occasions that may not be specifically in honor of the bridal couple. Intimate dinners in relatives' and friends' homes are a pleasant way to welcome the newcomer into the circle of friendship.

Q: *Though my future in-laws are warm people, I feel self-conscious when addressing them by name. My parents are the only ones I can sincerely call Mom and Dad, so right now I use Mr. and Mrs., but what do I do after the wedding?*

If formal address is a custom in your or your fiancé's background, then Mr. and Mrs. are appropriate.

Until your marriage, you could call them by their surnames unless they suggest otherwise. Later, you might ask your future in-laws what their preferences are. In time you will feel like a member of your husband's family, and addressing them in more affectionate terms will come naturally.

However, your in-laws might be puzzled if you call them Mr. and Mrs. when the rest of their daughters- or sons-in-law use warmer expressions. What if they called you "Mrs. Smith?"

Lovers, Young or Mature

Q: *I would like some information on the purchase of an engagement ring. Does a man buy the ring beforehand? What options do I have if the diamond is too expensive? Who chooses the wedding bands and when? Etiquette books seem to be written for women. What about the groom's role?*

In your letter you don't mention whether you have parents. The engagement period is an important time when both sets of parents are brought together. Unlike in times past, your role is to be part of the decision making, so join your bride and her family in discussions. But you should also remember that the financial burden may be wholly on the bride and her parents, so temper your point of view. There are many unpredictable problems that arise; all you can do is to meet each step as it comes along.

You must have a wedding ring for the ceremony, but an engagement ring is not needed to be engaged to be married. A remembrance of the time you decided to marry can be something the bride will cherish nevertheless. If this is not the right time for such an expenditure, just let it go for now. There are always occasions to gather those other trappings.

If you want to ask her to marry you with the ring in your pocket, then do so, but make sure the ring can be exchanged. After you know what is on the market and how much jewelry costs, then you and your fiancée should go shopping together.

- A diamond set in platinum is the top of the line; set in gold is somewhat less. There are endless choices, including the bride's birthstone. Other choices are a pearl, opal, ruby, amethyst, topaz, turquoise, tourmaline, and others not necessarily thought of as engagement stones.
- Bridegroom: If you shop alone, be sure the receipt states the ring is taken "on approval." It might be lovely but not to your fiancée's taste. She might like a matching set.
- The engagement ring of the matching set is worn above the wedding band.
- Rings can be adjusted to size.
- After you know what is on the market and the cost of jewelry, then you both make the selection. If you decide on matching wedding bands, then this is the time to buy them.

The value of a diamond depends on a number of factors.

- *Clarity:* Most diamonds have natural flaws, but these imperfections should not hamper the flow of light through the stone.
- *Carat* or *Karat:* A unit weight for measuring precious gems. There are a hundred points to one carat, and a one-carat stone is the size of a plump pea.
- *Color:* Most diamonds are a transparent white with a touch of color—blue, yellow, pink.
- *Cut:* Traditional solitaire shapes—round, square, heart, pear, marquis, and oval—are still the most popular. It is the best investment.
- *Cost:* The Diamond Information Center says the average couple spends at least two months' salary on a diamond engagement ring.
- *Coverage:* Insure precious gems under a separate rider, not under an overall homeowner's policy. Appraisal is given by the jeweler and updated periodically.
- *Care:* The stone can chip. Remove the ring when washing hands or dishes because the gem can loosen in its setting. Always put it in the same safe place at home.
- Your jeweler can advise how to keep the diamond sparkling clean.

Like gold, diamonds can be used as international barter and always retain *a* value. When I say "retain *a* value," I mean that the value may go up or down in the marketplace.

My Betrothed, My Fiancé(e)

Q: What is the correct pronunciation for the words "fiancé" (male) and "fiancée" (female)? I was corrected the other day when I referred to my future husband as my "fiancé," which rhymes with "dance." I maintained that only the woman is known as a "fiance-SAY."

The word sounds the same for both genders: "fee-on-SAY." This French word is the only one I can think of that perfectly fits the state of being engaged to be married. "My boyfriend" sounds juvenile to me. Though I am particularly fond of the word "betrothed," it doesn't flow as smoothly in everyday conversation; it's the sort of word better read than said.

Engagement and Wedding Announcements

Q: Are printed engagement announcements sent out by mail out of style? I'm a working mother and it would save time from the cumbersome task of writing notes to so many out-of-town people.

Engraved or printed engagement announcements are considered inappropriate because a message is sent that can be misinterpreted.

The difference with a *published newspaper* item is that it is read by the general public but doesn't single out individuals who might infer that an invitation to the wedding will be forthcoming, which may not be so. Also, some people don't realize that there is no obligation to send a present upon knowing of or receiving an engagement announcement.

You might consider having wedding announcements in the hometown newspapers where you and your family grew up.

STOP THE PRESSES . . . WE'RE GETTING MARRIED!

. . . But, before you do, check the facts thoroughly. Nothing annoys a person more than seeing his or her name appear incorrectly spelled in the newspaper.

The bridegroom's family mails pertinent information to the bride's family. If given over the telephone, do not take anything for granted—code each name: GRANT—G as in George; R as in Richard, etc. Give schools and organizations their legal designation: U of M, in place of the University of Maryland, just will not do. Few establishments are as easily recognized by initials as the CIA or IRS. You would not want to have the reader puzzling over your story—it is not a classified ad.

Call or write the newspaper for their policy and request a form, or send the information, typed, double spaced, and in duplicate. A signature, along with your address and daytime (business) and home telephone numbers, as well as the principals involved, is needed for verification purposes.

Ladies and Gentlemen, here is a confession from *The Washington Post*'s Bridal Desk. Let us call it I'll Never Forget What's-His-Name.

A woman sent a notice to the Bridal Desk, spelling her future son-in-law's name incorrectly. Even though I checked it with her by telephone, she did not realize the error. She called back, saying how upsetting it was that a newspaper could make such a serious mistake. When I went over the copy she had sent, she blithely cooed, "Oh, Mrs. Gruen, I'll tell him you did it, anyway!"

Sporting of her, eh?

WORDING OF THE ENGAGEMENT ANNOUNCEMENT

Mr. and Mrs. James Person Ode of Washington, D.C., are pleased to announce the engagement of their daughter, Jill Candace, to Frederick Eldon Hampenstance, son of Mr. and Mrs. Harold Dean Hampenstance of Darien, Conn.

Miss/Ms. Ode will be a June bride.

You might want to add schools and places of employment:

Miss Ode is a graduate of the College of William and Mary and is currently studying for a master's degree in business administration at the Wharton School of Business and Finance of the University of Pennsylvania, from which Mr. Hampenstance received both baccalaureate and master's degrees. He is now with the management consulting firm of Smart, Smart and Certane Lee Smarter in New York City.

Ladies and Gentlemen, I prefer "is pleased to announce" or "take pleasure in announcing" to the use of "joyfully," which should be reserved for enthusiastic conversation.

Other identifying information about both families includes names of grandparents, parents' business connections, organizations to which the engaged couple belong, and the bride's debut. Newspapers will edit if they do not have space for the entire article.

DON'T BE SHY

A word to those who might feel self-conscious about the lack of clubs or ancestors going back to the Ice Age. Not only is your announcement interesting news to those you know, but it also makes the page interesting to readers. You are part of the building blocks of society, and the announcement takes a special place in your memory book.

HONESTY IS THE BEST POLICY

An announcement should be truthful. Exaggerated claims of position or education can backfire and may have embarrassing results. It is better to omit rather than invent or inflate information.

FORGOTTEN PARENTS

Occasionally the bride's parents commit a faux pas by omitting the names of the bridegroom's parents in the text sent to newspapers, and the omission can be compounded even more if both families live in the same city. Most of the time the bridal

editor catches the omission, however. It generally is an over-
sight, not a slight, because the wording on most formal wedding invitations does not include the bridegroom's parents. If
the error is caught in time, fax the corrected version to the
newspaper(s) immediately.

It is a gamble to assume that others will not see the news
release, especially in newspapers that reach readers both na-
tionally and internationally. Case in point: An engagement announcement was placed by a young woman who was meeting
her prospective father-in-law in Cairo, Egypt, on the Wednesday the announcement appeared. When she landed, there was
the gentleman waving *The Washington Post*'s Wedding and Engagement page.

- Deceased in-laws are identified in the announcement, and
  the copy should make clear that they are no longer living.
- A widowed father or mother should mention his or her
  deceased spouse's name in the story:

  Miss Ode is also the daughter of the late Mrs./Mr. Ode . . .

- A remarried mother uses her current husband's name and
  may announce alone or with her husband. Include the future bride's full name and the bride's deceased father's full
  name:

  Mrs. William Williams
  OR
  Mr. and Mrs. William Williams of Vienna, Va. announce the
  engagement of her daughter, Jill Candace Ode, daughter of
  the late James Person Ode . . .

- If the bride's mother and stepfather have been married for
  many years or if the relationship is close, then the words
  "their daughter" can be substituted for "her daughter."
- A widowed father includes his deceased wife's given,
  maiden, and married names:

Mr. James Person Ode of Washington, D.C., announces the engagement of *his* daughter . . . Miss Ode is also the daughter of the late Sarah Manning Ode . . .

- A remarried father announces along with his wife:

  Mr. and Mrs. James Person Ode of Washington, D.C., announce the engagement of his (or their) daughter . . .

- If the bride's mother uses her married name but also is known by her professional name, she either identifies herself within the article:

  The bride's mother is known professionally as . . .

  OR

  Mrs. James Person Ode (her professional name)

- Separated parents, no matter the duration, are legally married and may announce as if they are still living together. They participate in all phases of the wedding.

- Friendly divorced parents announce jointly:

  Mrs. William Williams of Vienna, Va., and Mr. James Person Ode of Washington, D.C., announce the engagement of their daughter . . .

- If the relationship between the bride's parents is strained and the bride lives with her mother, the announcement reads:

  Mrs. William Williams of Vienna, Va., announces the engagement of her daughter, Jill Candace Ode . . . is also the daughter of Mr. James Person Ode of Washington, D.C.

- If the bride's father is doing the honors, her mother's name is mentioned:

  Miss Ode is also the daughter of Mrs. William Williams of Vienna, Va.

- When the announcement for the future bride falls to her brother, sister, grandparents, another relative, or close friend:

    Mr. and Mrs. Jeremy Person Ode of Chevy Chase, Md., announce the engagement of his sister . . .

- Whether her parents are divorced, living, or deceased, they are mentioned in the story.

HAPPY NEWS, SAD MOMENTS

Q: An engagement announcement is supposed to be a happy news item. Why mention my mother, who died last year? The thought of reading "the late" in the paper would make my father and me, and everyone who knew her, very sad.

Life is bittersweet. It is understandable that you miss your mother more than ever now that you're being married. But if you don't include your mother, the omission just leaves the reader wondering whether the parent died or ran away or if the omission is due to a nasty divorce. Make a clear statement. Even when there are bitter feelings between divorced parents or between parent and child, newspapers identify the principals.

If you can picture yourself reading the clipping a few years from today, you'll be so glad that, by sharing the news of her daughter's engagement, you brought your mother to mind again in a special way.

Ladies and Gentlemen, "the late" seems to some a cold way of saying the person has died, but it is uniformly used. The other choices—"is deceased," or, as some say, "passed away"—have the same effect: someone has died. Changing a word does not change the hurt.

MARRIED BUT OTHERWISE ENGAGED

Q: *My mother won't announce my engagement publicly because my fiancé's divorce isn't going to be final until the end of June. But this is my first marriage and I've read that it's the bride's status that counts, not the bridegroom's. She says that it isn't so in this case. Isn't she wrong?*

It's true that the bride's status determines what type of wedding is planned and that it doesn't matter how many times the bridegroom has walked the path to matrimony. But your mother is right: a public announcement is tasteless before the divorce becomes final—to say nothing about the legal ramifications. What do you think his associates, his family, and his acquaintances will make of a news story that says he is marrying again when the divorce isn't final? Waiting will save you and your family from embarrassing questions.

DISAPPROVING PARENTS

Ladies and Gentlemen, the young man's voice on the phone sounded frustrated. Though he has his parents' support, his fiancée's parents disapprove of their upcoming marriage because their daughter is too young. They will not participate in or attend the wedding and have forbidden their daughter to use their names in the engagement or marriage announcements for the newspaper. He wanted to know why they cannot name her parents without their permission since all they will be doing is stating the truth!

It is the truth, but the newspaper will not use her parents' names without their permission. I encouraged him to hold off. Her parents might soften by the wedding day, but to make that possible they must not antagonize them further.

TIMING OF THE ENGAGEMENT ANNOUNCEMENT

Some people announce when the couple becomes engaged because they wish to make known that these two people are pledged to each other, even if wedding plans are nine months to a year away. Others feel that an engagement is a statement of intent that may be broken, so the announcement is made public between three to six months before the wedding.

> Mr. and Mrs. James Person Ode of Washington, D.C., announce that their daughter, Jill Candace, will marry Frederick Eldon Hampenstance, son of Mr. and Mrs. Harold Dean Hampenstance of Darien, Conn., on the tenth of June.

HONOR NOT THYSELF

One never refers to one's self as "the honorable" since that term is only used when a person entitled to that respect is introduced in person or addressed by letter.

When the bride's father has a title, it is better to use the name that identifies the reason the person received the honor:

> Judge and Mrs. Miles Steptoe of Darien, Conn., announce the engagement . . .

Further in the copy, identify the judge's professional affiliation:

> . . . to James Rand Singleton, son of the Honorable Roland Sand Singleton, Judge of the Circuit Court of Appeals, and Mrs. Singleton of . . .

COUPLE ANNOUNCING FOR THEMSELVES

Though there is no age limit on having one's parents announce for the bridal couple, they may wish to make their own statement as part of the process of handling the entire wedding and reception.

> The engagement between Jill Candace Ode to Frederick Eldon Hampenstance is announced. The future bride, daughter of Mr. and Mrs. James Person Ode of Washington, D.C., holds the position of . . .
>
> Mr. Hampenstance is the son of Mr. and Mrs. Harold Dean Hampenstance of Darien, Conn. . . . etc.

FORTHCOMING
SECOND-MARRIAGE ANNOUNCEMENT

Jill Ode Hampenstance and William Jones Westings plan to marry in June. The future bride, daughter of Mrs. James Person Ode of . . . is Director of . . . Mr. Westings is Manager of the Division . . . etc. His mother, Mrs. Edward Westings, resides in Savannah, Ga. . . . etc.

NEWSPAPER MARRIAGE ITEM

The marriage of Jill Candace Ode to Frederick Eldon Hampenstance took place last Saturday afternoon in St. Bartholomew's Church in this city. The Reverend Marion Peaceful officiated at the double-ring ceremony. A reception followed at the Jockey Club. The bride is the daughter of Mr. and Mrs. James Person Ode of Washington, D.C. Mr. Hampenstance is the son of Mr. and Mrs. Harold Dean Hampenstance of Darien, Conn.

After a wedding trip to France, the couple will live in Manhattan.

Few newspapers print descriptive information, because they simply do not have the space. However, if you have an optimistic nature . . .

- The bride wore a Bianchi creation of silk taffeta . . .
- Her attendants were . . .
- Serving the bridegroom were . . .
- Her debut
- Bride's and bridegroom's degrees
- The couple's business connections
- Both fathers' and mothers' business connections
- Descendants of . . .
- Honeymoon trip and city in which they live

SOCIAL OR SOCIETY?

Q: In my day, newspapers published only those wedding and engagement notices sent by people who were considered society. When my engagement made the newspapers it meant a recognition of my family's place in the city. Is that true today?

Some papers were and still are "selective," which means the family wishing to announce must be prominent in some way. Other newspapers have discontinued publishing wedding and engagement announcements altogether. There are magazines that have the selective policy as well.

I have spoken to a number of newspaper people throughout the country and most, especially smaller dailies, tell me that all one has to do is mail a signed statement. They will telephone for verification, and the paper will use the announcement on a space-available basis. It is hardly treated as society news.

Once, the fact the bride and bridegroom had attended private schools and colleges was a legitimate basis for publication, an indication that the family had position. Nowadays, it is difficult for newspapers to make such obvious distinctions when we have a strong middle class and an expanding population. Only the famous or infamous, not necessarily members of "society," are covered strictly as news items.

Some papers charge for the announcement notices, which is

also the case in the United Kingdom. Only the royal family receives unsolicited coverage.

LADY LUCK SMILES

Two of my favorite announcements, which came to my desk a few years ago, illustrate my point:

The mother of the bridegroom placed her son's wedding announcement. He had just established a firm in an area of engineering new to the industry. A million-dollar deal came his way because his business attracted a Navy man who read the story. He telephoned the young man because that specialty was exactly what the Navy needed.

One of my most treasured letters of thanks is from a young lady who had recently married and was making her home in Washington, D.C. She said that her deceased grandfather, an African-American minister, had been a civil rights activist in the 1960s. He had marched with Martin Luther King, Jr., and was also the first black minister to give the convocation at the Republican National Convention. The engagement announcement made a huge splash. She received telephone calls and letters from people who had known her grandfather. They had no idea that his granddaughter was in the area.

Q: *I am the mother of the future groom. The mother of the bride agreed to send our son's engagement notice to my hometown newspaper, which she apparently didn't do. Doesn't the bride's family handle these matters any longer and is it acceptable for me to send it in?*

You don't have to rely on her family for the engagement announcement, if you know that it is appearing in the bride's hometown paper, or if you discussed the notice with the bride saying that you would like to handle the news yourself. Send the information to your paper.

However, the *marriage* announcement does not have to be announced by either set of parents.

Ladies and Gentlemen, at one time the bride's family sent the engagement or marriage announcement to the newspapers. The bride's mother asked the bridegroom's mother for family background information and mailed the story to the various newspapers, so the item appeared in all dailies the same day.

It becomes a sensitive problem for the bride's parents upon learning that the announcement they sent to the bridegroom's hometown newspaper charges to publish it. The bride's mother, living in a place where announcements are seen as news items, may object to such an expense in a city not important to her family, so she advises the newspaper to verify it with the bridegroom's family—an appropriate suggestion.

In days of yore, it was necessary for the safety of an unmarried young lady to come under the protection of parents or a guardian, since she had no legal rights. When the young woman married, her husband became her protector and the keeper of her fortune.

Today it is less rigid than in the past because some families share in every aspect of the event. However, many will retain the traditional customs.

The custom has been part of the engagement process—the bride's parents do the announcing and issue the wedding invitations in their names. The newspaper items and the wedding invitations are in their names. There is more leeway with the wording of the marriage announcement:

In the Great Choir of the Washington Cathedral in Washington, D.C., Jill Candace Ode became the bride of Frederick Eldon Hampenstance with the Reverend Jonathan Jardy conducting the double-ring ceremony. The bride is the daughter of Mr. and Mrs. James Person Ode of this city, and Mr. Hampenstance is the son of Mr. and Mrs. Harold Dean Hampenstance of Darien, Conn. . . .

If the bride's parents announce the marriage, then the wording begins with their names and the copy information above would need rearranging.

The content of the story is up to the person sending in the information, but it is the newspaper that makes the decision on the amount of the background copy and how it is written:

GUIDELINES
- Full maiden name of the bride
- Full name of her parents
- Addresses and home and daytime telephone numbers of both families for verification purposes
- Full name of the bridegroom
- Full name of his parents
- Date of the wedding
- Grandparents
- Schools and organizations
- Employment and, if you wish, position

For the wedding announcement, include all or some of the above and add:

- Maiden name of the bride
- Name of the bridegroom
- Where the event took place
- Name of the officiant
- Name of both sets of parents and where they live
- Description of the wedding gown (optional)
- Names of the bridal party (optional)
- Reception site
- Wedding trip
- Where the couple will live

PHOTOGRAPHS FOR THE NEWSPAPER

Q: My mother says it is customary to have only the future bride's photograph in the newspaper. My fiancé and I would like to have a picture taken together. Why isn't it considered appropriate?

It may be that the events from engagement to the wedding day are centered on the bride, or that marriage is a permanent change in status and hence more newsworthy, while the engagement can be severed without legal steps.

I do know, however, that today a picture of both partners is extremely popular with many young couples, both sets of parents, and with readers. Gone are the days when the bridegroom was a minor actor who hardly participated in the various aspects of this special event in his life.

Ladies and Gentlemen, want to know a secret? Well, I'm going to confess anyway. It seems that I am the culprit who broke the taboo about having the engaged couple's photograph in the paper.

In the late seventies, when touring in Spain with a group of fellow employees, a young executive told me that he wanted to be part of the newspaper photograph with his fiancée. Since I had heard that statement from other men, his comment convinced me. It is now accepted.

PHOTO REQUIREMENTS

Most newspapers require a 5" × 7" or 8" × 10" black-and-white glossy. Check the newspaper's policy.

Tape name(s) on the bottom of the photograph or write on the back with a very light hand so that the pencil impression does not show on the print side—that ensures identification should it become separated from the letter. Since newspapers do not guarantee the return of the photograph, enclose a stamped, self-addressed envelope.

For a successful couple pose, have your heads fairly close together so that the newspaper can "crop and scale" the print to fit their own specifications. A photograph of two people standing shoulder to shoulder would be difficult to reduce to the narrow columns in some newspapers. Avoid a dramatic or too-romantic pose.

Broken Engagement

Below is a repeat of a conversation I had with a young man that made quite an impression on me.

Q: When I became engaged to a young lady six months ago, my friends were not particularly enthusiastic, but I would not allow them to interfere. Just between you and me, she had bouts of temper and I finally came to realize that whatever feelings I had for her lessened with every tantrum, so I broke the engagement. Somehow I did not expect to fend off inquisitive questions from friends. Why do I have to give an explanation?

Friends should be more discreet, but maybe they wanted to hear you say they were right. Try a little humor. My father tells this parable about a man who had a difficult wife. When friends would ask what the trouble was between them, he would answer: "I never talk about my wife." He lived in misery until the children left home, then he decided to divorce her. When the papers became final, his friends asked him: "Now that you are no longer living with that woman, can you tell us what was wrong between you?" He answered: "I'm sorry, but I never talk about strangers."

Ladies and Gentlemen, rare is the man who wants to play Shakespeare's Petruchio to an ill-natured Katharina. In *The Taming of the Shrew*, Petruchio takes over the task of subduing Katharina's volatile character, recognizing that her behavior was a cry for recognition. And rare is the person who possesses the insight to a complex human being—to know the difference between a psychologically disturbed individual and someone sending a message.

I looked up the word "shrew," which, in this sense, means an ill-tempered woman. However, my fellow females, I could not find the male equivalent of the word. So, since I believe in equality of the sexes, I have designated an ill-tempered man as a "shrow." The dictionary term is "a scold, a shrew." A shrow can be likened to the Tasmanian devil, an animal about the size of a badger that growls and will fight anything in sight—even a stick. . . .

Now, where was I? Oh, yes, we were talking about broken engagements. Lovers are generally on their best behavior during courtship. Conscious of what pleases the other, they try to anticipate each other's needs. Surely there is something dreadfully wrong when there are frequent bouts of temper and uncontrolled diatribes—a rather strange way to woo one's beloved. Do not confuse those tantrums with one nervous outburst during the planning stages of the wedding—it is hard being cool all the time when working or studying, partying, and trying to keep up with all the hundred and one things that need doing.

It is important that couples meet each other's friends as well as family, even though our unwilling Petruchio might not have agreed with me had I said this at the time of our conversation. Not all favorite friends on either side will be compatible, but compatibility is important in a relationship. Friends enrich life, and if one partner has always been sociable and the other almost a recluse, a hard adjustment will result. However, if these differences are not too extreme, two such different temperaments can end up being a good balance.

RETRACTION OF NEWS STORY

Q: *We announced our daughter's engagement in the newspaper. Now that it is broken, do you think we ought to have a statement published to that effect?*

The wording of the newspaper announcement is a simple statement:

> Mr. and Mrs. James Person Ode announce that the engagement between their daughter, Jill Candace, and Frederick Eldon Hampenstance, son of Mr. and Mrs. Harold Dean Hampenstance, has been broken by mutual consent.

In most cases, I would just let the news flow by word of mouth. It is advisable only if the reason for notifying is compelling.

There is always an "on the other hand" for wanting a retraction of this kind. Let us suppose that because you were not keen on your daughter's choice, you wish it to be known to as many people as possible that the alliance is severed. It might be hard to resist a public statement, since you cannot stand on a rooftop and yell "Yippee!"

Ladies and Gentlemen, this subject needs commenting upon. Most couples, on the surface at least, want to make a clean sweep since a broken engagement is unencumbered by marriage. The breakup can be terribly upsetting—possibly more so for one side than the other—but there should be certain "sporting" attitudes.

First, the couple should not vilify each other; remember, there must have been love in the beginning or the engagement would never have taken place. All expensive presents exchanged between the couple over the engagement period ought to be returned, as well as any intimate correspondence—

though now in the days of lazy letter writers it seems highly unlikely that many couples will have a problem in that area.

Second, if there is an established household or an apartment full of furnishings, then the dismantling and the decisions about ownership are more involved. Sometimes a disinterested third party can be of help, but be sure that person really is impartial.

Engagement and wedding gifts from family and friends are also returned to donors.

Prepare and Enrich

Marry 'em first and change 'em later is the biggest darn fool trap of the betrothal period. Few people are manipulative or shrewd enough to play that game successfully throughout married life. For most people it is a shaky step to take toward the most important decision in one's life.

When a couple fall in love, they may make certain assumptions about their relationship. He assumes that the object of his passion thinks and reacts the same way he does. She is reluctant, however, to bring up subjects that might cause arguments. As the relationship deepens and the couple begin to talk about marriage, topics are avoided that might mar this idyllic time of courtship.

He tells her that he is not interested in having children; she does not say anything. He does not realize it now, she thinks to herself, but once we have been married for a time he will change his mind. However, she missed an extremely important clue and was grieved to find, after a few years, that he really meant what he said. She may have married him anyway, but had they discussed the topic before marriage she would have known what a chance she was taking.

After a few years of marriage, a couple had their first child. Suddenly, the fact that she was Catholic and he was not became very important. When they got married in a Catholic ceremony, the Church expected her to raise their children as

Catholics. It was not a signed agreement with the parish church but an obligation on her part, though not on his. Previously, when a Catholic married a person of another faith, the non-Catholic had to agree in writing that their children would be reared in the Catholic faith.

From the moment he saw his child, the father experienced a reawakening of his religious heritage and was not willing to allow his wife complete control of their child's religious education. "The child should know about both his parents' beliefs," he stated, "so that when he's grown up he can decide for himself." "You knew the implications when we had a Catholic ceremony. It didn't seem to matter to you," she protested. "I just didn't realize it," he responded. Both admitted that it had never occurred to them that their attitudes might change. They really expected to marry and be eternally happy without ever having to come to terms with their different religious beliefs.

Religious institutions, recognizing the high rate of unhappy unions and analyzing troubled areas in marriage, insist that the couple take part in marriage-counseling sessions.

For premarital counseling, many ministers of all faiths and counselors use the *Prepare and Enrich* research program that was developed by psychologist and scientist Dave Olson, Ph.D., and colleagues at the Department of Family Social Science at the University of Minnesota.

There are one hundred and twenty-five questions that each partner answers separately. The answers help the betrothed couple and their counselor to develop the couple's awareness of each other.

Couples learn what they can expect from each other in the future; they come to an understanding of whether or not they agree on vital issues. They may discover that much separates them, in spite of their strong physical attraction. Some find their love so strong that they are willing to adjust and compromise. Others realize that they knew all along that they are well suited and had no difficulty discussing the sensitive subjects others so adeptly sidestepped. Their relationship deepened.

ENGAGEMENT GUIDELINE
- Traditionally, the mother of the bridegroom telephones or writes the bride-elect's mother.
- If the bridegroom's mother does not call, the bride's mother should.
- Together they arrange to meet. If wedding arrangements will be discussed, then only the principals are present.
- If the bridegroom's divorced parents are friendly, they may be included in the initial meeting. If not, invite the mother of the bridegroom first, and later the father.
- An engagement party is generally hosted by her parents.
- An engagement ring is optional.
- The correct pronunciation of "fiancé" (male) and "fiancée" (female) is "fee-on-SAY."
- Printed engagement announcements mailed to individuals are inappropriate.
- Newspaper items:
    Telephone or write publications for policy and request forms.
    Type double space, in duplicate.
    Include addresses and daytime (business) and home telephone numbers of all the principals for verification purposes.
    Attach signatures.
    Include a stamped, self-addressed envelope for return of the photograph.
    Be sure information and spelling are correct.
- Wording of the engagement announcement: Include names of both sets of parents, deceased parents, and divorced parents.
- Timing of the engagement announcement: three to six months.

- Marriage announcements are optional. They are mailed soon after the day of the wedding and only to those who were not invited to the event.
- The newspaper photograph should be a 5" × 7" or 8" × 11" black-and-white. Tape name(s) on the bottom of the photo in case it separates from the form.
- Broken engagement: Return expensive gifts.
- Prepare and Enrich.

Gifts

To Give or Not to Give . . .

*T*hat is the question. Would you believe that some people want to put the words "No gifts, please" somewhere on the wedding invitations? They feel self-conscious about accepting gifts or seeming as if they expect them. Gift giving is customary and reaches back into mankind's beginnings.

Og, walking through the woods near his cave after a day of hunting, picks a few flowers for the dining-room table. His new bride will smile at this civilized gesture. Iggle was kidnapped from her tribe by the indelicate hair-dragging method of the day, which was the way sturdy young cavemen obtained brides. She constantly talks about her people from the north country, who are infinitely more cultured than his people; they are even into two-syllable words.

Suddenly Og hears a sound; he swings about. Standing before him is a stranger holding a club. Instinctively, he hands the flowers to the stranger, who eagerly accepts them, along with an invitation to supper. Our cave dweller returns to Iggle, who graciously accepts the bouquet from the traveler. She throws Og a triumphant look designed to show him that the stranger's behavior is the ultimate in the new-wave etiquette that has now resulted in a beautiful friendship.

And so we learn from our venerable ancestors that gifts are tokens of goodwill, of affection, of commitment, and that it is fun to give and fun to receive.

If some guests struggle with embarrassment about accepting gifts, there are others who face confusion about the when, what, and how of gift giving.

Does a lavish wedding entail an expensive wedding gift? No. One assumes that those hosting the wedding can afford the cost of the function they arrange. Even if they have stretched their budget, finances are not the responsibility of those invited to the wedding. Presents, as well as weddings, should be within one's means.

A late-nineteenth-century book on etiquette has a very strange suggestion. Everyone who sends a present should be invited to the wedding, but not all who are asked to the wedding are expected to give one!

Other than close family and friends, there is no obligation to give an engagement gift. People invited to the engagement party are those who will receive wedding invitations and be involved in prewedding parties, such as showers, which do involve gifts. Some families invite people not on the guest list because they are unable to invite them to the wedding. Doing so sends a confusing message, so I suggest that the first arrangement is more appropriate, unless there is a good reason to do otherwise.

Gifts, even those from the bridegroom's side, go to the bride's home before the wedding. A relative of the bridegroom might want to give him a check or a special gift in person, however. After the wedding, gifts go either to the bridal couple's home or to her parents'.

Who Sent What and When?

The bride-elect can keep her sanity intact by maintaining a record of gifts as they arrive. Few brides, no matter how clearheaded, recall who gave what.

Record the name of the sender: what he or she gave, the date the gift arrived, and the mailing date of the thank-you note.

Close relatives—parents, grandparents, aunts and uncles, and very close friends of the prospective bride's and bridegroom's families—give engagement gifts.

Some people take a gift only if there is an engagement party.

Engagement gifts remain unopened at the party and put in another room. A check is handed discreetly to the future bride or bridegroom but left unopened, unless given in private.

If you think that some guests might bring gifts to the *wedding* reception, have a cloth-covered gift table set up. The gifts remain unopened and are not given personally to the bridal couple. Checks remain unopened and are given to the bride's father or the best man for safekeeping.

For those who wish to give the future bride an engagement gift, the choices are wide open—items that are either personal or practical:

> Lingerie
> Jewelry
> Scarves
> Linens
> Bar implements
> Wine cooler
> Champagne
> Bread-baking machine (currently in vogue)
> Cuisinart

Iggle would have loved the last two suggestions.

Gifts of Money

There is the perennial question of whether money is an appropriate gift, though people are less rigid today about the issue.

Some people think it inappropriate to give monetary gifts. To them it is if they are making a judgment about the financial status of the bridal couple and their families. They send a gift that the couple can hold, use, and remember the donor with.

Others feel comfortable that the bridal couple will appreciate the chance to use the cash for a useful purpose. They might still be in school, furnishing a bare dwelling, or stationed overseas so that storing gifts may be a problem.

Just a word about gift certificates versus money gifts. Some people tell me that gift certificates limit the bridal couple to one store and that they would prefer to bank or spend the check where and whenever they please. Others say they dislike giving money because it shows no imagination or thought to gift giving—a gift certificate is in the same class as money.

An Eastern European custom practiced in this country is putting money gifts into the bride's wedding apron, or paying to dance with either the bride or bridegroom.

Often one hears suggestions through the grapevine about what the couple prefers. Such information is helpful, but the decision is the donor's to make.

Wedding gifts sent after the wedding are addressed to the couple's home, if they have returned from their wedding trip. If the couple expects to be away for a while, send them to her parent's home.

Young people should give something within their means, perhaps from the bridal registry, and not concern themselves with whether a certain monetary amount is adequate.

Checks are made out in the bride's name before the wedding and sent to her home address: Jill Candace Ode. To the couple it would read: Jill Candace Ode and Frederick Eldon Hampenstance or Jill Ode and/or Frederick Hampenstance.

Occasionally, a close relative of the bride or bridegroom might write the check to either one.

After the wedding, checks are written to Mr. and Mrs., or, if the bride has retained her maiden name, write both names.

What is the average amount people spend on wedding gifts is another recurring question. The answer varies from salesperson to salesperson in department stores. One gift registry specialist told me between two hundred to two hundred and fifty dollars. When checking with many people, some thought that figure inflated and others said it was about right. My observations were not illuminating.

One young woman was buying a single crystal wine goblet,

which then cost at least forty-five dollars. The occasion was a shower for the bride. "What will you give as a wedding gift?" I asked. She had not decided whether she would add a place setting to the couple's sterling silver flatware or the formal dinner set. Another woman, shopping for a wedding gift, bought a crystal pitcher for about ninety dollars and was pleased with her find.

Q: I'm invited to the ceremony and not to the wedding reception. Do I have to give a gift whether or not I attend?

No obligation to give a gift is attached to a ceremony-only invitation, whether you attend or not.

I would feel more comfortable giving something if I worked closely with the bride or bridegroom on a daily basis. However, if a neighbor casually asks me to attend the ceremony, I would think about it.

Joint Wedding Gift

Q: I'm a single person who, with my friends (two married couples), sent a joint wedding gift to a mutual friend. I thought it a good idea but they divided the cost by three, making my part of the obligation the same as theirs. It was more than I could afford. Any comments?

It would have been better for you if you had talked frankly before you agreed to the suggestion.

Some single people reason that a restaurant check is divided into fifths when dining out with married couples. Other individuals say they divide the cost into thirds since they would have spent about the same amount anyway. It is a matter of perception.

Q: I'm in the store sending a gift to my future daughter-in-law. I'm phoning you to ask how I sign my name—Mom, Mrs., or my full name?

Just sign your given name and surname but use a term such as "affectionately" to indicate a feeling of warmth.

Q: What would you consider a suitable wedding gift for my future daughter-in-law?

It needn't necessarily be something new, but something you feel would be unique as a remembrance of the first present you gave to welcome her into your family. In addition, she might be amused by your son's lock of baby hair, the bronze baby shoe, or his bear-rug bare-baby photo—that'll please him no end!

Q: What would you consider a suitable wedding gift for a son and his wife?

I've had many questions on the when, what, and if of gift giving but never what parents think fit to give their own children. How can anyone else make such a judgment? Though some parents are wealthy, they might give much less than others who spend much more than they should, given their circumstances. Attitudes toward gift giving are selective, and a lifetime of raising a child leads him or her to have certain expectations, whether reasonable or not.

Fun and the Bridal Registry

One of the tender memories the engaged couple will recall in future years is the time they chose the setup of their household.

Do not let the advice on what constitutes a fine set of silver flatware be daunting. It is good to know how to evaluate these things, for you never know what fortune has in store for you.

Often it is not what you have that counts but how you use it. Learning to set a table, the art of listening, interesting conversation, and serving even the simplest though well-prepared foods in an inviting manner are the elements that will build a reputation of refinement and cordial hospitality.

Window-shop before registering and, when you know your choices, make an appointment with the specialist at the bridal registry. Registering does not mean that people have to buy only what is on the list.

You should think about everyday flatware, glasses, and dishes as well as fine china, silver pieces, and crystal, along with other practical household goods. It gives people a greater range of choices for wedding gifts.

An established couple, who have been married before, may be reluctant to register. However, guests would appreciate knowing that a serving spoon or gravy boat would be a perfect gift.

STERLING-SILVER FLATWARE

Sterling-silver flatware is the most expensive and the most handsome.

Some fortunate couples start out with complete sets of fine china, crystal stemware, and sterling-silver flatware given to them as wedding gifts by close members of their families. Others gather them as the years go by, using special occasions to fill in, when they are able, with either a single piece or a place setting.

When shopping for crystal, china, or flatware, call your favorite store and ask when their most knowledgeable salesperson will be on duty and make an appointment.

The ideal number of place settings is twelve, since most dinner parties consist of eight, ten, or twelve people. An eight-piece place setting is the next choice. However, more than one young couple begins with a starter set of four, though six is more useful.

A basic place setting consists of four pieces:

Dinner fork
Salad fork
Knife
Teaspoon

However, five-piece settings are the most common.

Additions:

Butter spreader(s)
Soup spoon
Meat-serving fork
Gravy spoon
Vegetable spoon
Large serving spoon
Fruit knives
Fruit forks
Sauce ladle
Cake knife
Pie server

Flat silver has an array of implements for every type of food one can think of—the odd pieces that are fun to collect over the years.

MONOGRAMMING OR INITIALING

Whether on silver or silver-plate, monogramming is not a simple decision as it once was. If silver is part of the bride's hope chest, bought as a gift on her sixteenth birthday, her maiden surname initial is etched on each piece and remains that way after she marries. If given as a wedding gift by a favorite aunt, her married surname initial(s) are used as the monogram.

Other choices may be the couple's given initials along with his surname initial.

If the bride has kept her maiden name, both sets of initials are used, one under the other.

There are books in the library that picture the different styles and typefaces.

SILVER-PLATED FLATWARE

Silver-plated flatware is rich-looking and not as expensive as sterling silver. The designs and patterns often are the same as those in sterling. Like sterling, silver plate is evaluated according to weight, balance, and the content of silver used. A well-made piece has a convex back or seam that gives the utensil more strength and can be monogrammed. Carefully examine the finish and the detail.

GUIDELINES
- Choose a reputable store that stands behind its merchandise. Be sure there is a guarantee or warranty.
- It is wise to have as many place settings in flatware as you have for china and crystal.
- Silver forks and spoons are well balanced if, when you place the curved part of the implement—where the stem meets the bowl—horizontally across your index finger, it rocks gently back and forth like a beam bar on a doctor's scale. It will fall if it is not weighted properly.
- The silver fork tines should be smooth and even.
- The knife handle is of silver and the blade of stainless steel.
- American silver has the name of the manufacturer and the word "sterling" on the back of the flatware.
- Old World pieces have a hallmark giving the country of

origin, the date of manufacture, and the quality of the silver.

- Style means classical, contemporary, or modern; the shape of the handle determines the shape of the bowl of the spoons and of the fork tines.
- Design is the pattern on the flatware. Some patterns have clean, simple lines, while others have intricate and ornately carved designs that hide scratches gathered over years of use.
- Ask the store about an airtight, tarnish-preventing silver chest to hold your flatware; it keeps the sulfur in the air from reaching the silver. Silverware-keeper kits are available to build into a silverware drawer that keeps the silver tarnish free.
- Hand-wash new silver or silver plate with soap and warm-to-hot water after using the first few times—it seasons the silver and rids it of the alloy that leaches out of the surface. The silver is then pure and reaches its full beauty.
- Reed and Barton advises that silver flatware may be safely washed in the dishwasher as long as no other metal implements are in the machine. It is not harmful to the utensils, except that it does create water marks on stainless steel.
- It is unnecessary to clean silver more than twice a year, especially if you use it often. Use a product like Hagerty polish and a nonabrasive natural ocean sponge. Rubbing with a soft cloth prevents scratches and keeps a lovely shine.

If you have the four- or five-piece table setting and your uncle in France sent a set of teaspoons, use them. Silver flat pieces do not have to match. If you have teaspoons instead of soup or dessert spoons, you can always add another pattern, whether its design is as ornate as yours or not.

STAINLESS STEEL

Stainless steel is preferred by some even though they can well afford to own the most expensive sterling-silver flatware. Stainless-steel flatware is less costly, unless you choose the top of the line. It has an appealing silvery-gray patina with designs ranging from modern to classic, even elaborately engraved. Be sure to use a dishwashing detergent that does not spot.

DINNER SETS

Like flatware, dinner sets are bought by the place setting:

Dinner plate
Salad plate
Bread-and-butter plate
Cup and saucer

Additions are:

Rimmed soup plate—also serves as a salad plate when it is being used for dessert
Luncheon plates
Serving platters
Vegetable and covered serving dishes
Soup tureen
Demitasse cups and saucers
Teapot
Coffeepot
Creamer and sugar bowl
Fruit or dessert bowls

It is best to start with two sets. Basic everyday dishes should be worry-free. Your dinner set for entertaining can be a style following that of your crystal and flatware, since you might like the same classic look in all three, or one can be more ornate than the others.

It is tempting to use the prettiest dishes every day, but save them for special occasions. You will enjoy setting a holiday table or having a dinner party knowing you have a complete dinner service.

Check what the words "open stock" mean. They used to mean that the manufacturer will produce that pattern for many years to come. It allows for future purchases of additional place settings or for the replacement of broken dishes. A "closeout" pattern might be attractive, but the chances of replacing pieces are next to futile.

The shape of the cup and the rim both should be as graceful to use as look at.

Bone china, translucent and delicate-looking, is generally the most expensive. Just as expensive and very handsome are dinner services with patterns of worldwide famous cities that are beautifully rendered.

Another choice is oven ware—oven-to-table dishes. Informal earthenware has a rich range of colors. If made by an artisan, each piece has a slightly different look.

For hand-crafted ceramic serving vessels, my sister-in-law—a ceramist—advises checking with the artist or vendor about whether the pieces are safe enough to hold food and are not just decorative. The vessels should be labeled on the back.

It is illegal to sell dishes made with paints that have lead in them. Though not tested, some glazes have high concentrates of substances such as barium that some ceramists feel are harmful over a period of time.

Also, ask the salesperson whether the pieces you are considering are dishwasher safe.

CRYSTAL AND GLASSWARE

The range of sizes considered necessary for a complete set of crystal differs. A basic starter set has:

Water goblet
Goblet for red wine

A goblet is a long-stemmed glass. When the choice is a two-piece set, choose the red-wine goblet because it is larger than the white-wine one and looks better balanced next to the water goblet.

Champagne in tall, narrow-rimmed champagne goblets holds its sparkle longer. The versatile wide-rimmed goblet doubles for custard or ice-cream desserts as well as for champagne.

Other additions to a set of crystal are the smaller V-shaped goblet for sherry and the short-stemmed brandy glass with its wide bowl and narrower rim. The smallest-sized liqueur glass, holding only two tablespoons of the sweeter, thicker aromatic spirits, is for an after-dinner drink.

A larger flat-bottomed glass has many uses, including holding both mixed and nonalcoholic drinks. The smaller size is for straight liquor or fruit juice.

Bridal Registry
and a Tale of Two Cities

An excellent suggestion from a mother of the bride planning her daughter's wedding is to register at a store that has a branch in the bridegroom's hometown. It made it so much easier for his people to choose from the bridal registry.

The store contacts the out-of-town one to request bridal registry information, even though they have no direct business with them. It is good public relations: the stores increase their sales, the bridal couple receive useful gifts, and the shopper is happy.

Exchanging Gifts

Q: It is impolite to exchange wedding gifts, but some are duplicates or completely useless items. We are starting from scratch—a tight budget. I feel like taking them back to the store and replacing them with things I need.

Exchanging gifts is a sensitive area and looked upon with raised eyebrows by some.

If you must do it, before returning the gifts think about diplomatically speaking to the donors—if they are close enough to you and you expect to entertain them in your home. However, it is different if you want to exchange gifts from people whom you barely know and do not expect to entertain. Exchanging duplicates is simple since no one need know whose gift was returned.

Rethink returning presents such as a cut-glass bowl. It may not be the most practical gift for your immediate needs, but it may be the start of the extra-fine serving pieces you will enjoy collecting for use in the future.

Lost Gift or Late Acknowledgment

Department stores keep excellent records, since they receive many inquiries about gifts they have sent out. If you check with the store and determine that the address is correct and the gift is recorded in their books as delivered, then it means the recipients have been tardy in sending their thanks. But if there is no record of delivery and the gift may be lost, explain the situation to the newlyweds by letter or telephone.

Ladies and Gentlemen, do not blame mothers for their children's tardiness. The most devoted of progenitors have some uncomfortable moments when asked if the gifts were received. All they can do is answer that the couple are delighted with the gift.

The bridal couple can seek help with the many things they have to do, but there are certain niceties that give a sense of caring and appreciation; one of these is a short, handwritten letter from either the bride or the bridegroom (yes, men can and do take pen in hand). Note the item received.

Cards with the words "THANK YOU" just will not do.

Thank-You Notes Before the Wedding

If the letter is to someone with whom you are not on a first-name basis, I suggest signing your name in full so that he or she will recognize the writer:

Dear Mr. and Mrs. Homer,

Frederick and I thank you for the salad-bowl set, which is on the counter looking handsome indeed. It is just what we wanted.

We are looking forward to seeing you at the wedding.

Sincerely,

Jill Candace (Ode)

Apart from "sincerely," other sign-off phrases are suitable, depending on the relationship—such as "affectionately," "as ever," "with love," "very sincerely," or "most sincerely."

When writing to relatives and friends close to you, picture them in your mind's eye and the words will come with warmth.

Dear Aggie and Johnnie,

    Fred and I can't wait to become hosts after our honeymoon so we can use the beautiful fruit bowl you sent us.

    As soon as we're back from Bermuda, we'll make a date. Meanwhile, see you two weeks from Saturday. Thanks from us both.

Love,

Jill

Better-Late-Than-Never Notes

Q: My husband and I, who married almost a year ago, haven't yet sent thank-you notes. We finally received the photo to be part of the thank-you card. Now I don't know how to word the note. Should I write an excuse? Also, is it all right to put the wedding date under the photo?

Just write your letter. Don't make any excuses or include the date of your marriage under the photograph. It would be a reminder that the thank-yous are late.

Q: I was married six months ago. Four guests have yet to send us the gifts they owe us. Should I send them reminder notes or confront them in person?

Gifts are *voluntarily* given. It would be inappropriate to ever bring up the subject. You will not endear yourself to those you confront and will most likely lose their friendship. For all you know, the gifts may be on their way right now.

If a gift was sent but is lost in the mail, the sender will wonder why he or she hasn't received a thank-you. They would probably telephone the store to have it traced.

Gestures of Appreciation

The bridal couple send letters of thanks to those who entertained them so graciously before the wedding.

Elopement

Elopement is not as common as it once was.

Occasionally the question is whether a gift is in order to a couple who were married secretly. It is appropriate if they are family members or close friends who would have been invited to the wedding had there been one. If you send a gift and later there is a reception for the couple, another gift is not expected.

Canceled Wedding

Her stepmother is in the throes of a dilemma. Her young stepdaughter, just as she was about to walk down the aisle, decided that she could not go through with the proceedings. The minister spoke to the bridal couple privately and recommended a postponement. The couple insist they will set another date though, so far, they have not. However, they want to hold on to the wedding presents.

The erstwhile bridal couple need not return the gifts if the postponement is for a short time. However, as long as six months is too extended a period, even if there is no serious difference between the couple.

Wedding gifts are exactly that and only sent and accepted on that presupposition. If too much time elapses, people will begin to wonder whether the marriage will take place at all.

Broken Engagement

He is perturbed on two counts. The young lady, after a long engagement, decided she did not want to marry him. The view of some regarding the engagement ring is that if his fiancée broke the engagement, she returns the ring; but she does not have to if he severed the relationship. However, this couple agreed they would return the more valuable gifts. He returned all the gifts by mail almost immediately. Time has elapsed, but she has not yet returned those he gave her.

Gift Timing

"When," asked a young voice over the telephone, "is it okay to give my friend a wedding gift?"

"Preferably," I answered, "after receiving the invitation to the wedding, but the time span is liberal since some people send gifts even six months after the event. When," I continued, as an afterthought, "is the wedding?"

"I don't know," was the answer, "I haven't received the invitation yet."

"In that case," I cautioned, "you ought to wait for the invitation before you send a gift because you wouldn't want to put yourself in the awkward position of assuming an invitation is forthcoming. Even the family might not know now how many guests they'll be able to include—not that receiving a wedding gift obligates the bridal couple to invite more guests than they are able to accommodate."

Ladies and Gentlemen, it may have been a coincidence but I received the following question shortly afterwards:

Q: We've a limited guest list and I find myself in the embarrassing position of receiving a wedding gift from a person I'd no intention of inviting. Do I have to invite her?

Even though you might feel uncomfortable about it, a wedding gift does not ensure a wedding invitation. Just send a thank-you note soon.

Second-Time-Around Gifts

Q: There is a sudden rash of second-time marriages that we'll be attending soon. I've read somewhere that two-timers aren't entitled to wedding gifts.

Two-timers? Are you sure you want to use that term? As a little girl in England, I learned from American films that the slang expression meant a person was double-crossing someone, or being unfaithful. The Chicago gangster, cigar hanging from his lips, rasped: "That two-timer! Rub her out!" (We both laughed.) "Oh, well, back to your question."

Some people take the stand that one wedding gift is sufficient, others not.

I think giving a gift is a way of celebrating friends' newfound happiness, knowing their unhappy experiences and more than a little bit of loneliness thrown in.

Opening and Displaying Gifts?

Displaying gifts has its sensitive aspects. Some brides feel it is a private matter between them and the donors. Conversely, there are families who feel that displaying gifts is a way of thanking guests for their generosity. Besides, people enjoy seeing the display.

It is easier to handle when the reception takes place at home or a place that is not trafficked by the public. Arrange a table covered with a cloth and decorated with ribbons in a room by itself so guests can wander in and admire the display. It is best not to identify donors if you have many duplicates or if you feel that some people will be a little self-conscious that their contributions do not compete well with the more expensive gifts. Checks are displayed with the sum covered by a strip of paper, allowing only the signature to show.

It is more involved at a hotel. Have a table in a corner area, so guests can place gifts on the table and the overflow goes on the floor. There is no obligation to open them during the celebration.

If the bridal couple wish a display table, assign a reliable person to look after it. The gifts are unwrapped and tastefully arranged, taking care to keep donors' cards and listing what they gave. Group those of like value so all the offerings look equally appealing. When the festivities are over, the gifts are rewrapped and transported home.

The British royal family displays all wedding gifts sometime after the wedding; the display is open to public viewing, as it was after Prince Charles and Diana, Princess of Wales, were married. The story is told that at the time Queen Elizabeth II married Prince Philip, an impoverished noblewoman sent an antique chess piece as a wedding gift to the royal couple that looked insignificant compared to the gifts of nations. The royal family exhibited it along with the thousands of other offerings by encasing it in glass with the legend: "This long-lost chess piece, given by ———, completes an antique chess set and is now one of the royal family's prized possessions."

Office Collections

Q: I work in a medium-sized office. The only time our department sees some fellow employees is when they take up a collection for something or other, especially wedding presents. Do I have to contribute to gifts for people I don't know? It's a steady flow of one donation after another, and some of these people are supervisors—it is intimidating.

You don't have to contribute to every manila envelope that comes your way. Some people find it hard to say no, even if no it should be. Others, no matter what is going on—even in their immediate office—have a general policy of refraining from contributing.

Management may be unaware that gift-giving is being over-done or that it happens at all and is a form of coercion. They should put a stop to the practice. Most offices keep collections within the area in which they work, and they should be on a *voluntary* basis. If the pressure is too politically strong, it is time to write a note for the suggestion box.

It used to be a rule of etiquette strictly adhered to by management and employees alike—gifts are not given to nor accepted by supervisors or those in management. They earn a good deal more than those under them. Even more undesirable is the appearance of currying favor or of intimidation. At the very least, gift giving can make people beholden in subtle ways.

I suggest that you and your immediate coworkers have a fund to which all equally contribute a small amount each week for those occasions. It may be that you would prefer going to lunch to celebrate and, if there is a sad time for someone, your fund could help.

Gifts for Attendants

Two of the most frequently asked questions are what are suitable gifts for bridesmaids and groomsmen and when are they given.

In the United Kingdom it is customary for the bridegroom to pay for gifts for the bridesmaids, as it once was in the United States. (How the change came about here I do not know.)

In this country the bride pays for her maids' gifts and the bridegroom for those who serve him. A gracious way of expressing appreciation, gifts should be personal and something that reminds them of the happy day they shared with the bridal couple. They do not have to be expensive. Some stores give a group price on several like pieces to encourage a purchase. I have not priced the gift suggestions below, and the choices in the marketplace are endless:

For Her Attendants:
- Silver necklace or wrist chain
- Bracelet
- Brooch
- Earrings
- Stick pin
- Silver or pewter picture frame
- Perfume bottle
- Hair ornament
- Miniature clock

For His Groomsmen:
- Business card holder
- Leather wallet
- Tie clasp
- Brass library embosser
- Bookends
- Travel clock

And so on . . .

Bridesmaids receive identical or almost identical gifts. However, the maid and matron of honor receive slightly more expensive gifts, as does the best man since their functions demand much more of their time than do the bridesmaids' and ushers'.

The amount of money spent is up to you.

Gifts from Attendants

The bridal luncheon is a good time to present the wedding gift to the bride, and the bride gives her gifts of appreciation to her attendants. The same goes for the groomsmen at the bachelor's dinner or if they are being entertained by him.

Gifts given to the bridal couple may be a joint one from all their attendants, or the bride's attendants may give her a separate present and the groomsmen buy a gift for the bridegroom.

Gifts Between Bride and Bridegroom

It is traditional in some families for the bridegroom to present his bride with a piece of jewelry, such as a string of pearls, on their wedding day, as it is for the husband to give his wife something when a child is born.

However, it is a private matter between the bridal couple and certainly not obligatory—establishing a home and taking a wedding trip are gifts in themselves.

Gifts to Parents

Before leaving on their wedding trip, some couples give tokens of love to their parents for their past nurturing, or they might wait until they reach their destination and send something special.

Guests

Who and How Many

*L*adies and Gentlemen, I have a confession to make. I've been avoiding the subject of the guest list. For a while the temptation was to work on a fictional story that had nothing to do with weddings, but that would have been the coward's way out. Anyone who can, in the most delicate way, tell a stepmom to "butt out" and Mrs. Ex-wife to give everyone breathing space is no coward—foolhardy, maybe, but not timorous. What is more, I now know why past books on weddings have adroitly avoided addressing the subject.

The bride's family, assuming they are the hosts, decide the number of guests to invite. The next step for the bride's family is whether they divide the guest list equally between both families or keep more invitations for themselves.

When the bridegroom's family want more guests than allotted to them, the bride's family might or might not acquiesce. A compromise might be that the bridegroom's side pays for their overflow.

Reasons the bride's family might refuse?

Money may not have a bearing on whether a wedding is small or large. Some people plan a wedding they can ill afford; others can have a lavish affair but it is just not their style. If the bride has a small family, they may want a balanced guest list—if they have fifty people and his side has a hundred and fifty, it would be overwhelmingly one-sided. The decision is up to the bride's family, if they are the hosts.

Practical hosts take a strong position by sticking to the guest list and the budget. They allot a certain number of guests for both sides of the family, and neither side may invite others in their place when regrets come in.

An old quip says: Rich or poor, it is good to have money.

When money is no object and the wedding planned is large enough to satisfy both families, everyone is happy. However, when the budget is tight some families have two lists; guests invited to the ceremony and reception and those invited to the ceremony only.

There are pro and con feelings about ceremony-only invitations. Some families feel uncomfortable about inviting people only to the ceremony, while others are uncomfortable leaving acquaintances out altogether.

Receiving a ceremony-only invitation pleases some people. The perplexed wonder, should I attend, and if I do, must I take a present? Others just send a card of congratulations.

Ceremony-only is an accepted practice in some communities who have an "open church." All are welcome, and a simple repast might take place in the fellowship hall after the wedding ceremony.

Ideally, the guest list should include relatives, friends, and parents' business associates on both sides of the family, along with the bridal couple's friends and business associates.

A bereaved person receives an invitation.

Now, when the word "relative" arises, where does the cutoff come—cousins, their children, or siblings' brothers- and sisters-in-law? It is probably best to start paring the list with the most distant relatives, such as the children of cousins. It may be that only the children of the bride's and bridegroom's immediate families are on the list.

There is no hard-and-fast rule, because it may be those second cousins, or cousins once removed, are friends as well as relatives. Does one chance omitting that second cousin's brothers or sisters, who are hardly known to the family but who would suppose that because a second cousin was invited all should have been? My friend invited everyone to her first son's wedding but the relationships remained distant. When her second son married, she only included the friendly second cousins.

Without hesitation, some people would invite friends over some relatives—friends who stood by them during difficult times. Others would not think of omitting any member of their family.

I remember a conversation with a woman who was offended when told that as much as her friends would miss her, they had a limited wedding-guest list. Only when her son married, and she faced the unenviable task of trimming the guest list, did she realize how tough those decisions are.

Inviting fellow employees and other business associates is a matter of judgment. If a person works in a small business where there is a measure of friendliness, an invitation to the wedding is appropriate. Those who work for a large organization do not generally invite its president to the wedding unless they are in top management. Inviting the manager of a large department might be feasible if the celebrant is a supervisor, but it is not even debatable if the office atmosphere is strictly businesslike and the hierarchy clearly defined. Inviting a person in a supervisory position along with close fellow workers, or all or part of the office staff, is a good decision.

There are career professionals whose lives are so structured that they have little contact with people outside business anyway. Using the invitation for political reasons does not always work but, on the other hand, it might cement a developing relationship.

Ladies and Gentlemen, the bride was married before and chooses a traditional small wedding. However, it is the bridegroom's first marriage and his family and friends are disappointed. Their reaction is understandable because the wedding ceremony is meaningful to those who are fond of him.

Guest List Pitfalls

Q: *As parents of the bridegroom, we have offered to pay for extra invitations because our family is so much larger and closer knit than the bride's. The other side agreed. However, every suggestion I make is politely ignored. My son says forget it. Am I wrong? After all, we are contributing.*

You are paying only for those over the amount you were allotted, and that fact does not invite you to make unsolicited suggestions.

Q: *Our daughter's wedding is taking place in three weeks. We allotted the groom's family sixty guests. They gave us eighty names; saying twenty of those would be unable to attend. Well, the "yes" responses are coming in. My wife can't sleep because even with sixty on our side and sixty on theirs we are over the budget. What is more, we are also almost twenty over the limit. What shall we do?*

You can't change the fact that you have a guest list approaching a hundred and sixty people—forty over the limit. It is improbable that 25 percent will be no-shows, since you have all those acceptances so far.

Maybe you can work something out with the bridegroom's family. Take it for granted that their twenty overflows are their responsibility. Without rancor, remind them that you limited them to sixty invitations. They might agree to pay for their extra guests, and you may discover that you and your wife are worrying needlessly.

Ladies and Gentlemen, there is a risk in inviting guests who you think will be unable to attend. The local person you are sure will be unable to attend because he works weekends, and could not possibly lose a day's pay, has found someone to exchange a working day with. You certainly did not expect your wife's aunt and uncle from Washington State to make the trip, especially since the aunt does not speak to most of her family. Suddenly, nothing will keep her from attending her beloved niece's wedding. After all, you invited her, and perhaps she sees it as an opportunity to make peace with her family.

You honor people when you invite them to your wedding, and they, in turn, honor you by accepting. However, the results are hard to face when your good nature overloads the guest list.

Another pitfall for well-meaning guests is to offer to pay for their children to attend the wedding. This puts the hosts in an embarrassing position. It is hardly likely, but suppose they did accept the offer and others closer to the family have been excluded. How would the hosts respond to the raised eyebrows? That the children were not on the original guest list?

Invitations

The Honour and the Pleasure

*A*fter you have wrestled and juggled with the guest list, the invitations now come to the fore. To cut down on the number of people to be invited, the family had to eliminate second cousins, which made no one happy but was unavoidable. And now the invitations . . .

The most handsome and expensive is the copperplate engraving. It is etched with fine line lettering and offers the widest choice of font (typeface).

Raised-letter printing on quality paper looks like engraving and is an acceptable substitute. Most people are unable to tell the difference, though raised lettering is usually sans serif (without decorative strokes).

The least-costly method is flat printing, on which the ink looks darker.

Though tastes differ, today's engravers or printers have examples of various styles and wording. The main components in choosing an invitation are appropriate wording, good-quality stock, the style of the printing, and the ink. For a formal wedding, most people want both traditional wording and traditional black ink on white or cream-colored paper. If preferences are conservative, traditional is the key to formal invitations.

Traditional Wedding Invitation

Mr. and Mrs. James Person Ode
request the honour* of your presence
at the marriage of their daughter
Jill Candace
to
Mr. Frederick Eldon Hampenstance
Saturday, the tenth of June
One thousand nineteen hundred ninety-five
at half after four o'clock
Trinity Church
New York, New York

Some people include the year, since the invitation is a keepsake for future generations to read. If all are invited to both the ceremony and reception, add:

and afterward at the reception
O R
a reception to follow
The Four Seasons
New York, New York

R.S.V.P.
O R
Please respond
O R
The favour of a reply is requested.

If there is more than one sponsor or host on the invitation, you will find under the "please respond" the name and address of the party assigned as keeper of acceptances and regrets.

---

* "The honour of your presence" indicates a religious service. "The pleasure of your company" is for social events.

The favour of a reply is requested.
Mr. and Mrs. Harold Dean Hampenstance
[Address]

RECEPTION CARD

Guests invited to the ceremony and the reception receive a reception card with the invitation. Ceremony-only invitations do not require a response.

Reception
immediately following the ceremony
at The Four Seasons
New York, New York

R.S.V.P.
[Address]

WHO IS THE SPONSOR?

Traditionally, no matter who is paying for the wedding, the bride's parents are her sponsors, and their names head the invitation. That formal custom has not changed, but the custom is not always followed.

DIVORCED PARENTS' JOINT INVITATIONS

The bride's mother uses her given name, her maiden name, and her ex-husband's surname.

Mrs. Sarah Manning Ode
and
Mr. James Person Ode
request the honour, etc. . . .
O R
Mrs. Sarah Ode

OR
[*Ms. Sarah Manning]

BRIDEGROOM'S PARENTS' NAMES ON INVITATION

When both the bride's parents and the bridegroom's parents share responsibilities for the wedding, the wording is:

Mr. and Mrs. James Ode
and
Mr. and Mrs. Harold Dean Hampenstance
request the honour of your presence
at the marriage of
Jill Candace Ode
to
Frederick Eldon Hampenstance
[etc.]
OR
at the marriage of their children
Jill Candace
and
Frederick Eldon
[etc.]

It is difficult for guests to identify whose wedding they are invited to when the parents of the bridegroom have a different name from his:

John Eric Hamilton
son of
Mr. and Mrs. Bartlett Samuel Silver

It is appropriate and a genial gesture to include the bridegroom's parents on all wedding invitations.

---

* If the bride's mother has taken back her maiden name.

Frederick Eldon Hampenstance
son of
Mr. and Mrs. Harold Dean Hampenstance
[etc.]

MARRIED BUT DIFFERENT NAMES

Q: The bridegroom's mother wants both her husband's and her name printed on separate lines because she has a Ph.D. and a hyphenated name and insists no one will know her. It is a formal invitation and it would be incorrect. Am I right?

That format is used when a couple is divorced or if the wife's name is completely different from her husband's. It is less confusing.

Avoid listing his parents' names under yours because it makes it seem as if they are cosponsoring the wedding.

Under the bridegroom's name, add:

son of
Mr. and Mrs. Harold Dean Hampenstance
(Dr. Sarah Eldon-Hampenstance)

The version below gives the impression that the bridegroom's parents are divorced.

Mr. Harold Dean Hampenstance
Dr. Sarah Eldon Hampenstance

I do not recommend it. Stand firm.

STEPFATHER

When the bride has her deceased father's surname and her stepfather is the only father she has known, the invitation reads:

Mr. and Mrs. Harold Holdern
request the honour of your presence
at the marriage
of their [or Mrs. Holdern's] daughter
Jessica Miles Troth

DOUBLE WEDDING

When parents host a double wedding for their daughters, the older daughter's name is first:

Mr. and Mrs. James Person Ode
request the honour of your presence
at the marriage of their daughters
Jill Candace
to
Mr. Frederick Eldon Hampenstance

and

Jocelyn Courtney
to
Mr. Seth Bertram Southall
[etc.]

Wording for cousins or friends would include both brides' parents:

Mr. and Mrs. James Person Ode
and
Mr. and Mrs. Wallace Tyne Guild
request the honour of your presence
at the marriage of their daughters
Jill Candace Ode
to
Mr. Frederick Eldon Hampenstance

and

Imogene Wallace Guild
to
Mr. Jonathan Wilde Hopewell
[etc.]

JOINT INVITATIONS

Q: We are about to order invitations to our wedding but are not sure just how to word them since my parents, his, and the two of us are sharing expenses.

I prefer the traditional style because the matter of sharing expenses need not be so specific. There is just so much one can say on an invitation:

Jill Candace Ode
and
Frederick Eldon Hampenstance
along with their parents
request the honour of your presence

However, there are less formally designed invitations that list the parents' names on either side of the single card. Centered are the names of the bridal couple and the rest of the information.

SINGLE PARENT

Traditionally, a widow uses her deceased husband's name:

Mrs. James Person Ode
requests the honour of your presence

Note the verb on the second line when a single name heads the invitation.

A widow with a professional name uses both:

Mrs. James Person Ode
(Millicent Fantastic)

When the bride is an actress or a professional person who uses a name other than the name she was born with:

Mr. and Mrs. James Person Ode
request the honour of your presence
at the marriage of their daughter
Jill Candace Ode
(Sandra Makebelieve)
to
[etc.]

DIVORCÉE

In the past, divorcées used their former husband's full name, "Mrs. James Person Ode," even though he was married to a woman who holds his name. Currently, a woman uses her given name (optional), maiden name, and ex-husband's surname. Some take back their maiden name, prefacing it with "Ms."

There is an ongoing debate whether divorcées, when reverting to their maiden names, should use "Mrs.," "Miss," or "Ms." "Ms." solves the problem. After all, whether a man has been married five times or is a widower, he is still "Mr." His title does not broadcast his history.

BRIDEGROOM'S PARENTS AS SPONSORS

When the bridegroom's parents sponsor the wedding, the invitations go out in the name of his parents:

> *Mr. and Mrs. Harold Dean Hampenstance*
> *request the honour of your presence*
> *at the marriage of*
> *Jill Candace Ode*
> *(daughter of)*
> *(Mr. and Mrs. James Person Ode)*
> *to their son*
> *Mr. Frederick Eldon Hampenstance*
> *[etc.]*

The prefix ("Miss" or "Ms.") is used if her parents are not included in the announcement.

OTHER RELATIONSHIPS

When relatives are the sponsors, identify the connection to the bride: "their sister," "granddaughter," or "niece."

There are three situations when the bride's prefix, "Miss" or "Ms.," is included: when the bride does not have parents to sponsor her, and a relative does the honors; when friends are acting as sponsors, but the phrase "their friend" would be omitted because it looks awkward; when the couple is giving the wedding.

> *Mr. and Mrs. George Manfred Semper*
> *request the honour of your presence*
> *at the marriage of*
> *Miss [Ms.] Jill Candace Ode*
> *to*
> *Mr. Frederick Eldon Hampenstance*
> *[etc.]*

COUPLE ISSUING THEIR OWN INVITATIONS

The honour of your presence
is requested at the marriage of
Miss [Ms.] Jill Candace Ode
to
Mr. Frederick Eldon Hampenstance
[etc.]
O R
Miss [Ms.] Jill Candace Ode
and
Mr. Frederick Eldon Hampenstance
invite you to their wedding
[etc.]

Please respond

Parents of a young widow or young divorcée sponsor their daughter; but in both cases the bride should use her given name, maiden name, and her deceased or former husband's surname:

Jill Ode Hampenstance

The above style is the same if a young widow or a divorcée issues her own invitations.

A mature widow, who is known by her late husband's name, issues her own invitations:

Mrs. Frederick Eldon Hampenstance

PRIVATE CEREMONY—RECEPTION ONLY

Sometimes a private ceremony takes place and a large reception follows or is given at another time. The reception invitation would be standard size and the ceremony-only one would be approximately 5" × 3¾".

Mr. and Mrs. James Person Ode
*request the pleasure of your company

If there is more than one sponsor or host on the invitation, list the name and address of the party assigned to keep track of acceptances and regrets under the R.S.V.P.

Only the people closest to the bride and groom attend the ceremony. Guests are invited in person, by letter, or telephone. Engraved invitations are unnecessary, unless there are more than fifty people or if the family wishes to do it.

DELAYED OR LATE RECEPTION INVITATIONS

If the couple eloped or were married elsewhere, both sets of parents might want to host a reception later:

In honour of
Mr. and Mrs. Frederick Eldon Hampenstance
Mr. and Mrs. James Person Ode
and
Mr. and Mrs. Harold Dean Hampenstance
*request the pleasure of your company
Saturday, the eighth of July
at half after seven o'clock
Hotel Pierre
Alexandria, Virginia

R.S.V.P.
1111 Reception Way
Alexandria, Virginia 22000

MILITARY BRIDE

Today, a military bride can use her rank and branch of service on formal wedding invitations, or have the civilian wording.

* Note the change of wording indicating a social event.

Mr. and Mrs. Jackson Lloyd Formand
request the honour of your presence
at the marriage
of their daughter
Janet Lesley Formand
Lieutenant, United States Air Force

It is the same for servicemen:

to
Frank Joseph Marlington
Lieutenant, United States Air Force

Informal Wedding Invitations

The wording should be clearly stated so that the recipients understand what they are invited to, so they can respond.

Mr. and Mrs. James Person Ode
invite you to witness
the exchange of marriage vows
between their daughter
Jill Candace
and
Mr. Frederick Eldon Hampenstance
son of
Mr. and Mrs. Harold Dean Hampenstance
on Saturday, the tenth of June
at noon
[etc.]

Bilingual Invitations

Bilingual invitations are not only gracious but practical, especially when the bride or bridegroom, though living in this country, was born in a foreign land. The invitation is in both languages. The English language is printed on the left side and the other language is on the right. The bridegroom's parents head their side of the invitation and the wording reads as if they are the sponsors.

Ecumenical Wedding Invitation

The pitfalls involving wedding invitations are not only whether the wedding is going to be formal or informal but also the subtle or not-so-subtle story that the wording reveals.

The future bride wants to include the priest's name as the officiating minister on the invitation. She is a Catholic marrying a Presbyterian, and her fiancé would not consent to marry in a Catholic church. They compromised. She agreed to the ceremony in his church with the priest co-officiating in the nuptial rites. When the time came to think about the invitations, she realized that the wording made it seem as if the entire wedding ceremony would be Presbyterian—held in the "Presbyterian Church" and with no mention of her denomination.

I could not offer a solution because the name of the officiating ministers appearing an the invitation would be most unusual.

Misprints

Misprints can happen. So before ordering wedding invitations, study the samples shown and do not make a decision until you feel comfortable with your choice.

There is a difference between *ordering* invitations with the modern "honor" instead of "honour" and a *misprint*. It is the customer's responsibility if the wording was ordered that way and overlooked when proofread. A misprinted word is the engraver's fault, and it is his responsibility to redo the invitations.

A word to professional engravers and printers: It would be

helpful if they discussed with the bridal couple the difference between the two words on a formal invitation.

Q: The bride's mother asked how I, a widow and the groom's mother, wish to have my name printed on the wedding invitation. It's going to be a white-tie affair, but instead of "Mr. and Mrs." on the first line of the formal invitations, they are going to have "Alden and Dorothy Saunders"—unheard of! Also, since my husband died not long ago, I would like the traditional widow's name and my recently deceased husband's name.

If they decide to use their first names, there is not much you can do about it. On the other hand, tell the bride's mother that you want to use your *formal* name and, though I have only once seen a deceased person's name on an invitation, I heartily approve—though a deceased person's name does not appear on the first line, as if sponsoring the wedding. It should read:

son of
Mrs. Bartlett Samuel Silver and the late Mr. Silver

However, a widow *heading* an invitation uses her formal name—"Mrs. James William Bentle." By the way, it is a custom in some countries to include a deceased parent's name on invitations.

Titles

MILITARY AND DIPLOMATIC TITLES

Titles are basic to protocol and etiquette, part of the discipline of diplomatic language to which organizations such as the diplomatic corps and the armed forces strictly adhere. Any deviation might be offensive, misread, or misunderstood.

When a person is the only one in that position, it is not necessary to write his or her name.

If you are not sure of a dignitary's title or how to address him or her, telephone the person's protocol office.

ESQUIRE/LAWYER

In this country, "esquire" is occasionally used by lawyers when conducting their business affairs. The word is not a social one or an earned title such as "doctor," "judge," or "justice."

HONORABLE

"The Honorable" is not used only when referring to one's self. If the mother or father of the bride is entitled to that honor and is issuing the invitation, use the professional title rather than "The Honorable":

Judge and Mrs. James Person Ode

However, on invitations naming the bridegroom's "honorable" father:

son of
The Honorable and Mrs. Harold Dean Hampenstance
[or his mother]
The Honorable Sarah Eldon Hampenstance
and
Mr. Harold Dean Hampenstance
O R
Mr. and Mrs. Harold Dean Hampenstance
(The Honorable Sarah Eldon Hampenstance)

It is traditional that on social occasions a woman uses her husband's name, even though she has a title of her own. Some women have no objection to the custom. Others feel their identity is important and prefer their titles—"Judge," "Doctor," "the Reverend,"—on all occasions, and that includes "Doctor" (or "Ph.D." after her name).

Traditionally, Ph.D. holders use the title for professional reasons only.

PHYSICIANS

The traditional wording is:

Dr. and Mrs. Wilson Stephens

Separate names:

Dr. Wilson Stephens and Dr. Millicent Stephens
OR
Drs. Wilson and Millicent Stephens

If she has retained her own name:

Dr. Millicent Wiltons
Dr. Wilson Stephens

If you are not sure how to address the envelope, a telephone call to his or her office will solve your dilemma.

A fourth-year medical student, who will graduate a few days before the wedding, uses "doctor" on the invitation—even if the invitations were ordered earlier.

MILITARY OFFICERS' RANKS—
SOCIAL OCCASIONS ONLY

The armed forces encompass all five services. I think of it as an umbrella term.

The Marines are part of naval services, though officer ranks are the same as in the Army and Air Force. The Navy and the Coast Guard have slightly different forms

*Navy and Coast Guard**
    Admiral and Mrs. Thomas Thomlinson
    Vice Admiral
    Rear Admiral
    Commodore
    Captain
    Commander
    Lieutenant Commander
    Lieutenant
    Lieutenant, Junior Grade
    Ensign
    Chief Warrant Officer
    Warrant Officer

All Other Branches
    General and Mrs. Thomas Thomlinson
    Lieutenant General
    Major General
    Brigadier General
    Colonel
    Lieutenant Colonel

* The Coast Guard is part of the Department of Transportation. It is also under the Uniform Code of Military Justice. It has peacetime missions, and has supported the other four services in wartime since 1790.

Major
Captain
First Lieutenant
Second Lieutenant

MILITARY DESIGNATION GUIDELINES
- The United States Air Force and the Marine Corps require full rank.
- The United States Army does not use the designation of "First" or "Second" before the word "Lieutenant."
- A retired military officer with the rank of lieutenant colonel or commander and above uses his rank and does not indicate that he is retired from the service on the wedding invitation.
- A widower announcing alone would indicate whether he was retired or not.
- Those with lower ranks would use "Mr."
- A reserve officer may use his rank on the invitations when on active duty. If not active, then "Mr." is appropriate.
- A medical doctor in the Navy uses his rank when he is a commander or above.
- A lieutenant commander or under is known as "Doctor."

CLERGY

Although each denomination has its own designation, the correct *written* terminology is "The Reverend."

The list below includes Episcopalian, Lutheran, Roman Catholic, Eastern Orthodox, Jewish, Mormon, Seventh-Day Adventist, Christian Scientists.

- *Episcopal:* The Reverend Doctor; The Reverend Doctor Presiding Bishop of Episcopal Church; The Right Reverend; Bishop of Episcopal Church; The Right Reverend Dean;

The Very Reverend Archdeacon; The Venerable Canon; The Reverend Canon
- *Lutheran:* Pastor
- *Presbyterian:* The Reverend
- *Baptist:* The Reverend
- *Methodist:* Pastor
- *Catholic Cardinal:* His Eminence, John, Cardinal Doe *Bishop and Archbishop:* The Most Reverend Abbot; The Right Reverend Monsignor; The Right Reverend Priest; The Reverend Father
- *Eastern Orthodox:* Archbishop; The Most Reverend Bishop; The Right Reverend Archimandrite or Priest; The Very Reverend
- *Jewish Rabbi:* Doctor or Rabbi (after obtaining the doctor of philosophy)
- *Mormon* (Church of Jesus Christ of Latter-Day Saints): Bishop
- *Seventh-Day Adventist Church:* Pastor
- *Christian Science:* Church of Christ, Scientist, is a lay church and does not have ordained ministers. Their members marry in other Christian churches.

Inner Envelopes

Q: I am sending invitations to everyone in the family, including grand-parents and aunts and uncles. It seems so cold to refer to them as Mr. and Mrs. on the inner envelopes.

Go warm and affectionate—so "Grandmother," "Grandfa-ther," and "Aunt" and "Uncle" it is.

MILITARY WOMEN

For *official* occasions:

In service life, when a woman with the rank of major marries a captain, a lower rank, her name and rank are first on the outer envelope. Her husband's name and rank are written below. Also, she will be first on the inner envelope.

On *social* occasions, the correct form is the traditional civilian one:

Captain and Mrs. Wilson Stephens

. . . and that designation is being challenged, as it is in the private sector.

A woman in the service who has retained her own name has the same leeway as a woman in civilian life.

Timing for Mailing Invitations and Return Responses

Wedding invitations are sent three to four weeks ahead of time, though four, five, and six weeks should be allowed for weddings whose guests include people coming from foreign countries.

Within ten days is the average time for responding.

Postponed or Canceled Weddings

There are many reasons why a wedding is postponed. The most common ones are sickness or the death of a close family member, or it might be that the bride or bridegroom is in the military and cannot participate in the proceedings.

Postponing a wedding before the invitations go out is comparatively easy. Inform those you invited personally; notify the rest in writing.

If the invitations are already engraved and a new date is set, change the date on the invitation by hand as neatly as you can and insert a handwritten note stating the date has been changed. It would read:

"Please note: The wedding date has been changed from ——— to ———."

If no new date is set, a formally worded engraved or printed card goes out:

> *Due to the death [or sickness] of* ———
> *[or offer no reason]*
> *Mr. and Mrs. James Person Ode*
> *announce that the marriage of their daughter*
> *Jill Candace*
> *to*
> *Mr. Frederick Eldon Hampenstance*
> *has been postponed*

If the invitations have been mailed, act quickly with telephone calls and Mailgrams—especially to those who live abroad. More than a month will give you time to have cards printed; if not, send handwritten letters.

> *The marriage of*
> *Jill Candace Ode*
> *to*
> *Frederick Eldon Hampenstance*
> *will not take place*
> *[has been canceled]*
> *[has been postponed]*
> *[has been indefinitely postponed]*

Invitation to the Bridegroom's Family

Q: *My daughter insists that I send the bridegroom's family an invitation. That's ridiculous—it's an insult to send an invitation to their own son's wedding; as if they needed one!*

The wedding invitation is sent to the bridegroom's family with a note saying you thought they would like to receive one through the mail as a keepsake and not because they need one to know they are invited to their son's wedding.

Those Who Receive

Everyone in the bridal party receives an invitation, as does the clergyperson if invited to the reception. Invitations go to fiancé(e)s of those in the bridal party and to those who are dating someone on a *steady basis.* Casual friends are not included.

. . . *AND GUEST*

Take care to evaluate the relationships between attendants and their sweethearts and use the phrase "and guest" with discretion—if the status is uncertain, make a telephone call.

A young lady's steady date was asked to be his friend's best man. They had been seeing one another for some time and expected to become engaged—an understanding that was part of the conversations with the future bride and bridegroom since the two couples double-dated often. The young lady did not receive a separate invitation but was listed on the inner envelope of the best man's invitation as "and guest." Why, she asked her sweetheart, wasn't she sent a separate invitation and, barring that, why was she referred to as "and guest" when they knew her name?

The first flush of anger had her thinking she would not attend the wedding. Her second, calmer reaction was that she would attend but not go to the prewedding celebrations.

Note the repercussions over the thoughtlessness of changing a close relationship to "and guest."

LIVING TOGETHER

A joint invitation for a couple living together:

Ms. Sylvia Sommers
Mr. George Gordon

The inner envelope should also have both names but omit given names.

GROUP INVITATION

Q: I am inviting the entire office to the church only. Do I have to send separate invitations?

The most efficient way is to put the invitation on the bulletin board noting the department in which you work.

Acceptances and Regrets

Formal wedding invitation responses are handwritten. Follow the invitation line for line using black or blue ink on good-quality paper:

> *Mr. and Mrs. Invited Guests*
> *accept with pleasure*
> *Mr. and Mrs. James Person Ode's*
> *kind invitation for*
> *Saturday, the tenth of June*
> *[time optional]*

It is unnecessary to repeat the entire invitation line for line, as was once demanded. Address the envelope to your host and hostess, a custom that differs from other social occasions when only the name of the hostess appears.

If one member on the invitation is able to attend but not the other, write the name of the person who is accepting on the first line:

> *Mrs. Invited Guest*
> *accepts with pleasure*
> *Mr. and Mrs. James Person Ode's*
> *kind invitation for*
> *[etc.]*
> *Mr. Invited Guest*
> *will be unable to attend*

Q: *How do I respond to a formally worded engraved wedding invitation from the bridal couple themselves? Also, whose name appears on the return envelope?*

Whether accepting or declining, the formal wording is:

> *Mr. and Mrs. Invited Guests*
> *accept with pleasure*
> *[or regret that they are unable to accept]*
> *Jill Candace Ode's*
> *and*
> *Frederick Eldon Hampenstance's*
> *kind invitation to*
> *their wedding ceremony and reception*
> *on the tenth of June*

If you are not sure whether or not the couple is living together, address the envelope to "Ms. Jill Candace Ode." You might discreetly call a friend or relative for the information.

WRITER'S CRAMP

Take hold of yourself! Forget your nervousness over writing in the third person. Answering a formal invitation line for line is the simplest way to accept or regret. No excuse—especially if declining is to retaliate for the time the bride ignored your sixth birthday party—unless you wish to give a reason. Think of it as a short note and a convenient way to respond:

Miss Sally Shy
accepts with pleasure
Mr. and Mrs. Host's
kind invitation for
[etc.]

Response or Answer Cards

Though handwritten responses are traditional, answer or response cards are—albeit with protestations of helplessness—a practical solution for busy hosts. These cards make it easier for recipients to reply, and are far outdistancing the handwritten ones in popularity.

The most elegant response card for a formal wedding is on fine, firm paper in the same shade as the invitation:

The favor of a reply is requested
before May 22.
M_____
_____ accept(s) _____ regret(s)

Another, less-formal style:

Mr. and Mrs. Barnetta
[surname only]
accept

regret
Please respond by May 22.

It repeats the surnames of *only those invited* and is less confusing than the response card that asks how many people will attend. To me, "Mr. and Mrs. Barnetta" adds up to two people.

Asking for the number of guests is confusing and might give the impression that others not listed on the inner envelope may attend the wedding if they wish, which is not so.

RÉPONDEZ S'IL VOUS PLAÎT

Q: *I am marrying into a socially prominent family. My fiancé's grandmother is a stickler for correctness and knows all about the dos and don'ts. I know she won't approve of response cards, but should I use them anyway? I am too busy to telephone people who can't write an acceptance or regret.*

Grandmother will not like the idea of response cards. She will probably say: "People should know how to respond to a social invitation. Response cards are rude since they assume that recipients of invitations do not know how to write."

First, I will let you in on a well-known secret: Some people are tardy about returning response cards. Whichever way you choose, you will probably have to telephone slackers.

The choice is either courtesy to your fiancé's grandmother or convenience to yourself. I would use the traditional handwritten letter for the sake of his family. About a week before the wedding, contact those on your side who haven't answered. Ask his mother to take care of the tardy in her family.

Ladies and Gentlemen, you see what trouble you cause when you do not answer an invitation on time?

Informal Response

Dear Jill,

John and I will be delighted to attend your wedding. Seeing you as a bride standing next to Frederick on your special day will make us very happy.

Love,
Sheila

Stuffing the Envelopes

The easiest way to stuff the wedding invitation envelope is to pretend you are the recipient. When opening the envelope, you first see the handwritten name(s) on the unsealed inner envelope. As you turn the ungummed envelope over to withdraw the contents, the engraved wording should face you.

The enclosures are put in front of or within the fold of the invitation so nothing is overlooked. Follow the same procedure for inserts in the single page invitation envelope.

Additions on the Wedding Invitations

Any additions on the wedding invitation—such as "no gifts," "no smoking," "no children," or "cash bar" are inappropriate.

There are now restrictions on smoking in public areas, and those who smoke generally know enough to disappear for a while.

Are We or Aren't We?

Q: I've received an engraved, formally worded invitation from out-of-town friends to attend their daughter's wedding. It's being held at a house of worship. The R.S.V.P. is listed at the bottom left-hand corner, but there is no mention of the reception. Does that mean we're invited to the ceremony only, or that there is not going to be a reception?

An R.S.V.P. on the invitation means there will be a reception after the ceremony and that you are invited to both. I presume that the reception will follow on the premises of the house of worship. However, try telephoning a friend or the house of worship to be sure.

Q: *What does it mean when an invitation to an out-of-town wedding is without a "please respond" or a response card? I sent a wedding present since I am the bride's great-aunt, though I'm trying to interpret to what I have been invited.*

I'm mystified also. As a close relative living out of town, it seems unlikely that you'd be invited to the ceremony only, though that's what the invitation indicates. My first inclination is to tell you to check the envelope, but the reception card would be hard to overlook. There is no other solution than to telephone your niece.

Ladies and Gentlemen, the caller spoke to her niece who said that she had not bothered to enclose the reception card because she was not expecting her aunt to make the trip.

I made no comment and thanked her for the feedback. Really, that was not nice, was it? Even if her family's intentions were good, they should not have made up their aunt's mind for her.

I think our gentle aunt's niece had a twinge of conscience. She has been making solicitous telephone calls to her relative ever since.

Invitation to Church Only . . .

Below is a question that I included in the introduction to this book because it is an example of a misleading query.

Q: *When invited to the ceremony and not to the reception, is it oblig-atory to attend?*

Ladies and Gentlemen, after a few minutes of discussion I found I was speaking to an employer's wife who had received a ceremony-only wedding invitation from an employee, a young man who had worked for the firm for years. Apparently Mr. and Mrs. Employer had entertained the young couple in their home and expected to be on the reception list. When the invitation arrived, they were surprised and confused to find they were among the people invited to the ceremony only. They were in a quandary and really did not want to attend, although they had decided to send a present.

I did not voice my opinion because it is not my place to cause any more resentment than is already apparent. I did, however, wonder to myself why the bridegroom or his bride would chance slighting his employer and wife like that. How could it promote goodwill?

The young man shrugged away his involvement in the de-cision by saying that the bride's side was responsible for the arrangements. He certainly was not looking after his own in-terests and is now in an awkward position. Being in love is no excuse for allowing a slight to one's employer. The young cou-ple must realize the worth of each other's business and per-sonal relationships, from which both benefit.

It bears repeating that relationships are established and re-inforced by recognizing subtle nuances, or destroyed by thoughtless actions.

Ladies and Gentlemen, the question of attending the ceremony only does come up at the Bridal Desk once in a while. The sound of the voice coming over the telephone can be quite fretful. Some feel that they are being told that their relationship with the families is not close enough to warrant being part of the celebration. Others merely want to know what is customary. Anyone arranging a wedding with a limited guest list faces the task of leaving people out that they truly would love to invite. It simply cannot be helped.

Love Me, Love My . . .

Talk about an embarrassing situation: When receiving the response card from Mr. and Mrs. Barnetta, the bride's family were dismayed to see on the response card that four people were coming—the couple and their two children. The inner envelope had listed "Mr. and Mrs. Barnetta." The bride had not invited any children. This is a sensitive situation.

The bride could telephone the Barnettas and say how much she treasured their friendship and how happy she is they will be able to come to the wedding, but she is unable to include anyone's children except those in the immediate family.

If the children are invited to the wedding, their names would appear on the inner envelope. So if their names are not included, the first instinct is to leave them home without investigating further. However, if there is reason to believe they are invited, and *it should be a strong reason,* speak to a member of the family. Say that it is a delicate question and it is fine either way, but are our children invited? That will avoid the possibility of causing embarrassment all around by taking the uninvited.

Marriage Announcements

Marriage announcement cards and the wedding invitations are ordered at the same time. The announcements are addressed before the wedding day and mailed as soon after the wedding as possible. They are not a must but are a useful way to notify a large group of friends, relatives, and acquaintances *who were not* invited to the event. They follow the same format as the invitations:

Mr. and Mrs. James Person Ode
have the honour of announcing
the marriage of
their daughter
Jill Candace
to
Mr. Frederick Eldon Hampenstance
Saturday, the tenth of June
One thousand nine hundred and ninety-five
[city optional]
O R
Mr. and Mrs. James Person Ode
and
Mr. and Mrs. Harold Dean Hampenstance
have the honour of announcing
the marriage of their children
[etc.]
O R
announce the marriage of
Jill Candace Ode
to
Frederick Eldon Hampenstance
[etc.]

Because the bridegroom did not fall out of the sky and land ready-made on the bride's doorstep, I prefer the second version above, since it is a complete announcement.

COUPLE ANNOUNCING

Jill Candace Ode
and
Frederick Eldon Hampenstance
announce their marriage
on Saturday, the tenth of June
One thousand nine hundred and ninety-five
in New York City

BRIDEGROOM'S PARENTS ANNOUNCING

Q: The bride's parents are not going to send wedding announcements. Is it permissible for the groom's parents to do so?

You and your husband aren't limited by an outdated custom that prevented the bridegroom's parents from sending marriage announcements in their name. It is a holdover from the days the bridegroom's parents were strictly invited guests—they and the bridegroom were just expected to show up. Who made up these rules, anyway?!?

> *Mr. and Mrs. Harold Dean Hampenstance*
> *announce the marriage*
> *of their son*
> *Frederick Eldon Hampenstance*
> *and*
> *Jill Candace Ode*
> *daughter of*
> *Mr. and Mrs. James Person Ode*
> *[etc.]*

DO-SOS AND NO-NOS

- The exact time the ceremony is to start is the way it appears on the wedding invitation. To do otherwise causes confusion—sometimes among the wedding party itself.
- Abbreviations are unacceptable on invitations. Every word and numeral is spelled out except "Mr.," "Mrs.," and "R.S.V.P." "Dr." or "Doctor," "Jr." or "Junior," "Sr." or "Senior" can be spelled either way.
- Nicknames are inappropriate, even if you are absolutely sure that no one will recognize your name. Most people realize that Bill is an abbreviation of William, and Meg is a shortened version of Margaret.
- Buy a block of festive-looking stamps at the post office so

that the outer envelope and the enclosure envelope match.

- Personal notes are never written on the invitation itself, including the words "no gifts," "no smoking," "cash bar."
- When you place the order, the engraver will give you the envelopes to address ahead of time, unless they are needed for engraving the return address on the flap. Calligraphy is popular now.
- Go over the guest list for misspellings of personal names, place names, and street numbers.
- Check all addresses to be sure that invitations, once mailed, will not go astray, especially ZIP code numbers.

The post office separates and redirects incorrect ZIP codes to another area for sorting, which causes a delay.

A ZIP code book is sold that covers every city and town in the United States. Also, there is one available on the counter in the post office for the use of the public.

- The return address, preferably in raised lettering, should be placed on the back flap of the envelope and be legible on the outer envelope. Stickers are used also, but . . .
- Order twenty-five more invitations than the actual guest count to allow for errors or to send to alternatives on your list should you receive some *early* refusals.
- Before the final printing, ask for a sample proof. Read the text and check the paper and the font (typeface). Have more than one person proofread to catch typographical errors.

Proofread *every* character on *every* line of the entire invitation and on the inserts such as the reception and answer cards. The eye expects to see words spelled correctly, so a misspelling can be easily overlooked.

Can you tell me what is wrong in the following?

Mr. and Mrs. James Person Ode
request the honour of your presence
at marriage of their daugther
Jill Candace . . .

On the third line, "the" was omitted and "daughter" was misspelled.

- Matching ink is used on the outer envelopes, but black ink is appropriate also.
- The inner envelope names only those you wish to come to the wedding: Mr. and Mrs.
- If you are asking very small children, list them on the inner envelope under their parents' names, according to age.
- Young people's names appear on the outer envelope under their parents' names.

> *Miss Jean Harper*
> O R
> *The Misses Harper*
> *Master Seth Harper*
> O R
> *The Messrs. Harper*

Those thirteen—it used to be sixteen—and over receive separate or joint invitations.

- Tissue sheets are rarely used for engraved invitations, since the drying process is faster than it used to be. They are unnecessary for printed ones.
- All invitations are mailed on the same day.
- Send invitations three to six weeks before the wedding.
- Invitations are sent to everyone—including parents of the bridegroom, members of the wedding party, the officiant and spouse (if friends)—as well as friends and relatives in mourning.
- Guests arrive about fifteen to twenty minutes before the scheduled time.
- Do not bring an uninvited guest because you feel lonesome attending without a companion. A wedding is not that type of social occasion.
- Guests who are engaged should ask the bride if it is pos-

sible to include fiancé(e)s. (The request should be granted.)
Send separate invitations unless there is a shortage; if not,
on the inner envelope, under the first name add:

Miss Betrothed
Mr. Treble

- Maps and enclosures are helpful and can be included with
  the invitation.
- Guests reply immediately to accept or decline the invitation. If there is no answer card, write your response by
  hand the formal way.
- Check your guest list for the correct spelling of personal
  names, as well as place names and street numbers.
- Correctly address the rank of those in the armed forces as
  well as the titles of the clergy and other titled personages
  —both in America and foreign countries.
- Stuffing wedding invitations.
- A deceased person's name never appears on the top line of
  the wedding invitation. Only the widow or widower does
  the sponsoring.
- An invitation should be clear to the recipient as to what
  he or she can expect. If the reception is to take place after
  the ceremony in the house of worship, add: "Reception
  following." However, those two words are not included
  on the "ceremony-only" invitation.

NEWSPAPER MARRIAGE ANNOUNCEMENT

Mr. and Mrs. James Person Ode of Washington, D.C., announce
the marriage of their daughter, Jill Candace, to Frederick Eldon
Hampenstance. The bride is Director of Second Chance, Inc.,
and Mr. Hampenstance is Vice President of the parent company
. . . etc. His parents, Mr. and Mrs. Harold Dean Hampenstance,
live in Darien, Conn.

Planning
the Wedding
and Expenses

$\mathcal{W}$ edding planning is a time for imagination stretching, a time to draw on one's talent for tact and diplomacy, a time for problem solving.

A wedding needs good organization skills that include hiring a bridal consultant, if affordable; topical reading; and seeking advice from friends who have gone through the experience. The mind's eye should walk through the proceedings step by step.

As the dazzling arrays of wedding plans continue, one can appreciate what it takes to arrange a diplomatic or political dinner, a business function, or a church affair honoring the bishop. While there are similarities, such occasions cannot match the emotional aspect of marrying.

The excitement of the engagement melds with practical matters. Find the most professional services available. Word-of-mouth recommendations are often the best. The least-experienced firm may charge only a little less or about the same as the most-competent one.

A wedding for a young couple revolves around parents, relatives, their friends, and their parents' friends. She might be completing undergraduate or graduate studies and living on campus. Her fiancé might recently have taken employment out-of-town. After doing the legwork, her mother telephones her findings to her daughter, who comes home on weekends or major holidays to rush about with her mother. In between time, the future bridegroom comes to town when he can take an extra day off.

An independent couple in their thirties who are in the midst of pursuing careers has solid friendships and a set lifestyle. Whether parents are paying for the wedding or not, the people invited are a balance of the couple's friends, along with business associates and family relations on both sides. They make their own wedding arrangements and parents generally take the position that it is completely up to the lovers' taste.

There are three questions to be answered before choosing the type of wedding to be planned. What degree of formality will it have? How much money can be spent? How large is the guest list?

It is unrealistic to plan *a very formal* wedding with a tight pocketbook. The key word is "very," and it is synonymous with more—a *more* expensive wedding dress and accessories, *more* invitations, a *more* elaborate reception, *more* attendants, which means *more* flowers and *more* money to be spent on presents. It would be a big mistake to suppose, as someone once said to me, "Budgets are made to be broken." That will cause headaches, not happiness.

Some couples choose a small, intimate wedding without business or social acquaintances, keeping the guest list to relatives and intimate friends.

Clergy

Choosing an officiant is generally the prerogative of the bride and her family. If the bridegroom's family wish their clergyperson to co-officiate, they talk to the bride's family, who discuss it with the officiant.

CLERGY'S FEE

The bridegroom generally pays for the officiant. Often people feel self-conscious about bringing up such a practical subject as payment. Not to worry; just telephone the secretary at the house of worship who, though reluctantly, suggests about fifty dollars. They are hesitant, as I am, about quoting an exact amount because the figure represents a stipend to the clergyman/woman or a donation to the church. It is up to the donor to decide what would be appropriate.

Some clerics, however, view the role of officiant at weddings as part of their ministering to the *members of their congregation,* and that includes counseling the couple before the wedding.

A qualifier: I do not know if all denominations have the same policy because some have split and formed their own churches.

In Jewish weddings, fees are paid to the rabbi and the cantor and are considered part of their income. Rabbis who do interfaith ceremonies are sometimes more expensive.

A clergyman/woman is often a co-officiant in a wedding ceremony, with a visiting officiant (such as the bridegroom's religious adviser) as an assistant—unless the visitor is a high-ranking personage such as a bishop. The donation still goes to the home minister, though a further contribution would be given to the other officiant. A friend who officiates receives a gift rather than a fee.

When the wedding takes place out of town, the family pays the officiant's traveling and lodging expenses. A friend might be sensitive about accepting expense money because he would have attended as a guest anyway. You could try to present him with a personal gift or a donation to his religious order.

ROLE OF THE OFFICIANT

An officiant is *not required* to perform a wedding ceremony if there are doubts about the circumstances. Officiants judge legality and propriety according to their conscience.

Propriety? Suppose either of the two young people is underage. They want to marry, but the officiant does not have parental consent. An important prerequisite is that both parties must be of sound mind and marrying of their own free will.

Legality? Among other causes, the license has expired; one or the other is already married; they are not of the same religion as the officiant, who is forbidden by his church to perform the ceremony.

Who May Marry?

Although restrictions might differ among various religions, there are areas that are closely linked.

Every state in America has its own marriage laws, some more stringent than others. All follow to one degree or another the prohibitions on who may marry.

Below is the list from the state of Maryland. It starts with the statement that a marriage must be between a man and a woman.

A man shall not marry:
  His grandmother
  His grandfather's wife
  His wife's grandmother
  His father's sister
  His mother's sister
  His mother
  His stepmother
  His wife's mother
  His daughter
  His wife's daughter
  His son's wife
  His sister
  His son's daughter
  His daughter's daughter
  His son's son's wife
  His daughter's son's wife
  His wife's son's daughter
  His wife's daughter's daughter
  His brother's daughter
  His sister's daughter

A woman shall not marry:
  Her grandfather
  Her grandmother's husband
  Her husband's grandfather
  Her father's brother
  Her mother's brother
  Her father
  Her stepfather
  Her husband's father
  Her son
  Her daughter's son
  Her husband's son
  Her daughter's husband
  Her brother
  Her son's son
  Her son's daughter's husband
  Her daughter's daughter's husband
  Her husband's son's son
  Her husband's daughter's son
  Her brother's son
  Her sister's son

The list of prohibitions is specific within each religion, as in civilian law, though with differences. Such marriages, to say the least, are void. You will notice that not only blood ties (consanguinity or kindred) but those related by marriage (affinity) are forbidden. If you are thinking of marrying a relative, it is wise to check with your religious adviser and with the marriage laws of the *state* and *country* in which you live. In Greece, for instance, because marriage is forbidden between children who have the same godparents, an adult may only assume the role of godparent to children of the same sex.

The union of close blood relatives is harmful to offspring when carried from one generation to another, because negative genes are reinforced. The constant intermarriage of the royal families of Europe caused a great sadness in the Russian royal family. Queen Alexandra (Queen Victoria's daughter) married her cousin Czar Nicholas; the only male heir she produced was born with hemophilia, a dreaded disease. The ancient Egyptians did not know of the danger. Pharaohs married their sisters, to ensure the line of succession within the family. Over the years the dynasties died out because, it is thought, their offspring could not survive such severe inbreeding.

Marriage License

A marriage license is a permit to marry. It authorizes that:

The couple are free to marry each other.
Papers proving a divorce or widowhood have been produced.
Both are of legal age according to that *county*'s laws. If not, parental consent must be obtained.
The necessary requirements, such as blood tests—where stipulated—have been complied with.

In England and Wales, the law is uniform—those under sixteen are not permitted to marry, and those under eighteen must have parental consent. In America, applicants below the age limit must obtain permission of both the state and parents or guardians, and the law varies from state to state. There is such a wide range of ages, from twelve to eighteen—usually younger for women than for men. Both need to know the current laws in the particular state in which they will marry.

The United States Government prints information booklets. To request pamphlets such as "Where to Write for Marriage Records" and "Where to Write for Divorce Records," contact:

Superintendent of Documents
Government Printing Office
Washington, DC 20402

As of this writing, only a handful of states do not require a blood test, and some insist on medical certificates.

Having obtained the marriage license, the engaged couple may exchange nuptial vows *within the life of the license* and *within the area* (the same county) where they received the license. An expired license is invalid, so an officiant cannot perform the ceremony before the marriage license becomes valid or after it has expired. It is noteworthy that, according to the law of Maryland, the marriage would be recognized but the officiant and the couple could be subject to the penalties of the law.

One of the differences in law among the states is in their recognition of common-law marriage—the couple are not legally married but have lived together for a number of years. A common-law marriage is not recognized in Maryland, yet if a couple have lived together in another state that recognizes this type of union, Maryland will accept the couple as married when they take up residency in the state.

SIGNING OF THE MARRIAGE LICENSE

After the nuptial exchange, the officiant, the bridal couple, and two witnesses sign the marriage certificate in triplicate—the document is proof that the marriage has taken place. The officiant sends a copy of the license to the state, another is mailed to the couple, and the third is for the officiant's file.

Civil Ceremony

Q: My fiancée and I are being married at the courthouse in a civil ceremony. My mother says it is a cold and impersonal way to get married, so we'd like to compose our own vows. Do you know if they allow it?

Cold and impersonal? It can compare neither with the excitement that builds up while planning a wedding nor with the traditional and emotional response of a ceremony that combines the beauty of pageantry and the intimate feeling of being surrounded by relatives and friends. But it does suit the needs of some people who don't want a fuss. It is short and simple and legal.

Telephone for information on whether they allow changes in the standard service. If they don't, maybe one of their clerks will make a "house call." The law varies from county to county and state to state. In Maryland's Montgomery County, there are no deviations from the nonreligious wording of the civil ceremony.

Ladies and Gentlemen, the ceremony takes place in the Marriage Room, which has about five rows of benches for guests. The Clerk of the Court asks the bride and bridegroom to sign the register. With backs to the company—a female witness on the bride's left and a male witness on the bridegroom's right—the bridal couple face the Clerk, who conducts the exchange of vows in a ceremony that lasts no more than several minutes. It can be a double, single, or no-ring ceremony. Some couples forgo the ring ceremony because they will be repeating the process in a house of worship at another time.

I understand that most couples wear smart daytime clothes and have at least two people accompanying them. The day I visited, I was asked to be the sole witness for one couple who came alone. For their no-ring ceremony, the bride wore a pair of jeans and a short denim jacket. They looked as if this were one of the errands they had to run that day and barely had time to accept my good wishes and those of the Clerk's. It was true! They were in the military and one was being transferred, so they were rushing back to base to process the papers.

Dilemmas

Q: My daughter has been living with a young man. Now they are getting married and she wants a wedding. How do you go about arranging a formal wedding under those circumstances? I am also receiving hints from my mother about the propriety of it all.

Not so long ago a couple living together was unthinkable, but today it isn't. No one, even the clergy, asks questions. Be happy that the couple have decided they want to spend the rest of their lives together. As for the reaction of friends and relatives, they will come and dance at the wedding.

Q: My son has decided to marry a girl he met at college whose background is different from ours. Up to the time we visited her parents I didn't realize how different suburban and rural people can be. Since then, I have been sick with worry about this wedding and have told my son I can't invite my family or my friends to it. The ceremony, an interfaith one, will be held in a motel reception room where guests will be seated at round dinner tables already set for dinner. The wedding party will walk down a center aisle and programs, like those used in church, will be distributed.

These arrangements are completely alien to any wedding I've attended but, to top it all off, at the reception there will be limited champagne, enough to toast the bridal couple, plenty of beer and wine, and if guests wish hard liquor, there will be a cash bar!

At that point I couldn't contain myself. When I objected to having guests pay for anything at a wedding, they said that the bar will be in another room so no one will see money change hands. Have you heard of such arrangements?

I feel the same way as you do about the inappropriateness of a cash bar, though it is not unusual in some areas; neither are programs for a church ceremony.

My suggestions might not be to her family's liking, just as you find their customs not to your taste. But they're hosting the wedding. The bridegroom's family involvement is limited in the wedding proceedings.

You will hurt your son if his family doesn't attend the wedding—it is his family as well as yours. Tell your people that they are going to a country wedding that is a bit different from what they are used to—it might be fun for everyone.

Ladies and Gentlemen, during a subsequent phone call with the young man's mother, I had a sudden feeling that the bride's family had put on the "we are hicks from the hills" act for the bridegroom's parents. If the young man's mother was worried and clearly thought the match unsuitable, it is possible the other side felt the same way. Her son seemed to be wavering.

Wedding Day—His Dreams and Hers

Ladies and Gentlemen, I find it fascinating to discover how people come to certain conclusions. Sweethearts decide to marry but each envisions the events of the wedding day in an opposite manner. Both have been married before—she, in a single-ring civil ceremony with a small reception at a restaurant. He was the resplendent bridegroom exchanging wedding rings with yards and yards of bridal illusion and calla lilies. Now she wants to look "bridey." Not, she promises him, that she will wear a veil and look like a floating virgin. They will invite everyone to the reception, she says enthusiastically. He, on the other hand, having gone through the whole bit, would like to marry quietly in a single-ring ceremony in a judge's office and later invite a few select people to wish them well.

Can you just see where they both are coming from? Having

had broken marriages, apparently not without scars, they do not want to have a wedding resembling what each had the first time.

One recurring theme that keeps drifting my way, and is a concern mainly between men and women—what if he suffers from male ringophobia *malade imaginaire* (or, in Latin, *sexus masculina*) disorder? While most men are comfortable wearing a wedding band, some men just do not like to wear jewelry and some women just do not like the idea that some men do not like to wear wedding bands.

Why, she asks, should I wear one if he does not? He says that the wearing of a ring by either sex does not promote constancy and that those who want to be unfaithful will not be deterred by a ring, unless, when fancy is tempted, it has some magical power to prod the conscience.

Ms. Ring might choose to wear a wedding band or not. However, women have a certain amount of protection from unwanted attention when they wear one—though only from those who seek a carefree relationship. Even a divorcée will suddenly sport a ring when it suits her purpose, and, just as she can produce one, he can secrete his away.

Unlike a tetanus shot, wearing a ring does not give anyone immunity from the "wandering desire virus," which can attack either sex.

The *exchange* of wedding rings is an integral part of Eastern Orthodox rites, but double-ring ceremonies in Protestant and in Jewish Conservative and Reform wedding ceremonies are a fairly recent introduction. It depends solely on choice and is not part of a religious belief or rite. The single-ring ceremony is still observed in Orthodox Jewish weddings since the ring is traditionally the symbol of something of value presented to the bride by the bridegroom. Its symbol is purity (of gold) and circular (unbroken). The giving of the ring was depicted by Egyptians over 4,500 years ago, and the ring was considered "earnest money"—a sign of good intentions.

SINGLE RING

One young bride felt that there was no point, perhaps even a hint of insincerity, in having a double-ring ceremony if he was reluctant about wearing a ring. To her, the vows were the most meaningful part of the ceremony. Besides, when she analyzed it, the single-ring ceremony was traditional and everything about their wedding was old-fashioned.

Sickness or Death in the Family

Q: *Although my father is ill, he insists we go ahead with the wedding as planned. Apart from the heartbreak, I am terrified that he may pass away at the time of the wedding or even on the wedding day. Do you know of others' experiences and how they handled it?*

At this bittersweet time, the decision to go ahead with the wedding is made by you and your side of the family, in consultation with your father's doctors and, if you wish, with the guidance of a religious adviser.

If your father is too ill to attend but is able to participate from the sick bed, it is possible to set up a speaker phone at the altar enabling him to hear the ceremony on a conference-call line. He may even be able to say a few words during or after the ceremony. That is how my family handled a similar situation.

Ladies and Gentlemen, there are gigantic feats of strength exhibited when the will overcomes the body so that the stricken person's wishes are fulfilled.

Two instances: A terminally ill father of the bride was too weak to move but insisted there must be a way he could attend his daughter's wedding. Two cousins took him into the shower until the warm water had loosened his pain-racked body enough to enable him to be dressed and ensconced in a wheelchair. At the reception he even tried dancing with his wife and his daughter. It was the best gift he could have given his family. As all can imagine, there was not a dry eye in the place.

It was deadline time at the Announcement Desk when I received a call from the mother of an engaged girl saying that it was important to have her daughter's engagement announcement in the newspaper's next insertion date. Her husband, though alert, was at death's door and knew it. He wanted to be able to read of his daughter's betrothal in *The Washington Post*, and he did.

After the gentleman died, his wife telephoned to say that the preparation of the wording, the expectation of reading it in the newspaper, and finally its appearance with a photograph of his daughter not only worked as a distraction but also gave him a sense of completion.

Conflicting Decisions

Q: We are planning a small but elegant wedding. Her parents are paying for the food, mine for the liquor and flowers, and my fiancée and I for the rest of the expenses. Suddenly there are little annoyances that are cropping up; the photographer, for instance, is much more expensive than we realized. Also there are differences in opinion about what constitutes an elegant wedding. I don't know what I expect you to say, but have you had any experience in this area?

Trouble begins when expenses exceed the budget and when six minds (three couples) must compromise. First, forget who's paying for what. Each couple lists the items they feel are important and the cost for those items. Listen to all sides, negotiate, then you and your fiancée make the decisions. You might want to divide the total expenses three ways.

Lodgings for Out-of-Town Guests

When the bride's family reserves a block of rooms for out-of-town guests, most hotels offer reduced rates. The hotel gives the bride a stack of pamphlets, and she mails them to guests. The rates are clearly stated, and guests are responsible for their accommodations. They make their own reservations.

Guests, when paying the bill, remind the checkout clerk that they are entitled to the reduced rates.

Bridal Couple Walking Together

Q: At our wedding ceremony, my fiancé and I are going to walk to the altar together. Do we hold hands or walk arm in arm, and am I on his left or right?

You walk, holding hands or arm in arm, on the left of your bridegroom.

Shivaree

Q: My fiancé has just told me he belongs to a club that follows the practice of serenading newlyweds on their wedding night. I think it is tacky and will feel extremely embarrassed by this show of attention at our hotel. What do I do?

Either you are funning me or he is teasing you. If what he says is true, *firmly* persuade him to keep the name of the hotel a secret from everyone, as newlyweds have done until recently.

Ladies and Gentlemen, I treated the question seriously but I think it was a put-on. The practice the young lady is referring to is a genteel equivalent of the old-fashioned "shivaree," a type of cat-and-mouse game.

In some rural areas it was the custom of townspeople to

guess where the bridal couple would spend their first night together (a quaint custom). They would surround the house while
banging on pots and pans, creating a frightfully discordant row,
and some managed to enter the bridal chamber.

Though the newlyweds tried to avoid the shivaree by keeping their hiding place a secret, it was a practically impossible
task in those days. Some couples were painfully sensitive about
the hazing; thicker skins knew full well that they had done it
to others and now it was their turn.

Everything the Couple Should Know

Whether yours is a formal or an informal wedding, the first
order of business is to satisfy the old bridal rhyme, to which,
with apologies to Mr. or Ms. Anonymous, I have added something new of my own in italics.

Something OLD—*a link with the past*
Something NEW—*a marriage to last*
Something BORROWED—*a friendship of giving*
Something BLUE—*a sky full of living*
And a SIXPENCE in your SHOE—*for good fortune*

So "old" can be an heirloom cameo; "new" might be a gift
of pearls; borrow your friend's lace wedding handkerchief, ac-
cent the underskirt of your dress with a blue ribbon . . . and a
shiny dime can be your English sixpence.

PLANNING GUIDELINES
- If the bridegroom's family intends to contribute toward
  some of the expenses, they should make the offer early.
- His family should give out the guest list as soon as possible.
- Have some alternative wedding dates and times of day
  from which to choose, apart from the one decided on by

all. The officiant, the house of worship, and the reception place have to be coordinated.

- Make an appointment with the officiant for marital counseling.

    Discuss the institution's guidelines for music and the proceedings of the wedding if you have major preferences in terms of the ceremony or the music.

- Keep records on file cards in alphabetical order; write the names of potential guests with their addresses, telephone numbers, and relationship to you.

- Names on the "absolutely sure" list are kept in one file, the "maybes" in another. When replies start coming in, meticulously enter the names on the cards. Separate acceptances and regrets.

    Record on the donors' cards the type of gift, arrival date, and when a thank-you note was sent.

    The file boxes, especially if painted a bright color, serve as silent reminders to keep up with notes of thanks.

- Once the bridal gown, veil, and accessories have been chosen, as well as the bridegroom's attire and accessories, choose the color scheme for members of the bridal party.

- The bride's mother chooses her dress first and the bridegroom's mother follows.

- Choose bridesmaids and groomsmen—the number is generally balanced, though not necessarily.

- Do not be shy about asking for help from honor attendants—that is their function.

- It is estimated that one usher is needed to escort fifty guests.

- Ask relatives and friends to put up out-of-town bridesmaids. If not, hotel expenses will be your responsibility.

- The bridegroom has the same responsibilities to his attendants.

- Arrange with a hotel to reserve a batch of rooms for out-of-town guests—at their expense.

- Photographer—hire a person with wedding experience.
- Announcements for newspapers are sent in a timely manner. Discuss having a black-and-white glossy print taken.
- Music—make an appointment with a band leader to hear the band play at a wedding. Pick the music for the ceremony and reception.
- Engravers—order invitations (add twenty-five over guest count), informal and formal cards, and wedding announcement cards.

    Carefully proofread the wording.
- Caterer: Check services and prices.
- Order the wedding cake and, if you will be having one, the bridegroom's cake.
- Florist: Now that you know your color scheme, select the floral arrangements.
- Discuss transportation from the ceremony to the reception and afterwards to the place where you will be staying that night.
- Discuss wedding-trip plans and the wardrobe needed for the climate. Make transportation and hotel reservations as early as possible.
- Plan transportation from the reception to your wedding-trip destination.
- Check all legal papers; driver's license.
- Make an appointment for fitting of the wedding dress; take wedding shoes to ensure that the dress will be the correct length. Have you worn the shoes in the house so they will be comfortable on the wedding day?
- Check with bridesmaids about their dress fittings.
- The bridegroom, his ushers, and the best man should go for their fittings. At the same time, the bridegroom orders accessories for his entourage.
- Choose wedding bands.
- Marriage license: Telephone the Marriage License Bureau for its policy.

- Plan bridesmaids' party, if you are giving one.
- Plan bachelor party—optional.
- Discuss guest list for rehearsal dinner.
- Judge the proper time to have haircuts so you will look just right on your wedding day.

  The bride: Take your veil to the hairdresser so your hair style and the veil complement each other.

  Have your nails manicured.

  Try a cosmetologist, but have a trial session to see how the makeup suits you—go for a natural look.
- Arrange rehearsal time for the wedding ceremony; notify the bridal party of the time and be sure to stress promptness.

  All should concentrate on their roles in an effort to achieve a smooth processional. The fun takes place later at the rehearsal dinner.
- Time the trip to the house of worship beforehand.
- Ushers receive the list of names of those who will receive special seating in the house of worship.
- Attendants should be enthusiastic about their friends' wedding plans—acting blasé just won't do.
- Best man: Remind the bridegroom to prepare the check for the officiant with a note of thanks.
- Choose going-away attire and wedding-trip wardrobe.
- Pack for your honeymoon.
- Traveling overseas? Are your passports up to date?

  Passport photographs are better in black and white than in color.

  The passport office has information pamphlets. They advise on the safety of the drinking water in foreign countries; inoculations needed; and location of American embassies and consulates.
- Change the bride's name on important papers—insurance policies, bank accounts, wills, etc.
- Travel tips: Leave expensive jewelry in the care of the hotel's or ship steward's safe-deposit box.

- Check dates and time for wedding and reception with florist, photographer, and band leader.
- Give the caterer a final guest count.
- You and your sweetheart should not let anyone interfere with your happiness. You are center stage so put on happy faces, even when pressures mount.
- Keep up with the thank-you notes.

The Wedding Day

Take a cue from Shakespeare:

All the world's a stage,
And all the men and women merely players . . .

Calm is the secret to a lovely bride and a relaxed bridegroom. What bride does not want to look serene when walking down the aisle; and what bridegroom does not envision himself the confident figure waiting for his bride at the altar?

Try to have all arrangements completed so that you have some free time to rest on the day before the wedding and an hour or two before dressing the day of the wedding.

Even though there is a rehearsal dinner the evening before the wedding, the dinner should end at a reasonable hour. For some bridal couples the wedding day starts early so that formal wedding photographs are taken when everyone looks fresh.

Check Your Lists: Do you have the
- License
- Wedding rings
- Toiletries
- Extra hosiery for the bride
- Sewing kit for an emergency
- Passports
- Tickets

- Car keys
- Money
- Charge cards

Remember:
- Apply all makeup and perfume and do nail repair *before* donning the wedding dress and shoes.

    Make sure that nail polish and deodorant are dry. My friend told me of a bride who walked down the aisle with tears streaming down her face because her wedding dress had a stark red splash of nail polish on the skirt.
- Keep sharp instruments away from clothing, especially stockings.
- If dressing away from home, be sure all containers such as lotions, nail polish and remover, makeup base, and face powder—everything that has a lid—*are tightly closed.* Pack these toiletries in a separate, securely closed case. Ziploc bags make excellent holders for items that are not self-contained because the opening closes as firmly as a zipper and they come in various sizes. However, be sure to check that the plastic bags are really closed.
- Whether prone to allergies or not, do not try new products right before the wedding. All experimenting is done at least a month before so that any adverse reaction to a new perfume or mascara will have disappeared by the wedding day.
- The above advice is useful to the bride. The bridegroom should be aware of the skin's reaction to a new shaving cream.
- If the bride is dressing at home, place a sheet over the seat and floor of the car to prevent soiling the wedding dress. During her walk to the car, she should lift her dress over her arm and straighten it when seated.
- The bride and bridegroom should mentally go through the main parts of the day:
- The bridegroom remembers to bring the marriage license and wedding ring.

- The bridegroom gives the ring to the best man.
- The maid of honor holds the bridegroom's ring.
- Everyone walks at a slow pace but not a crawl.
- Heads and backs should be straight, expressions pleasing.
- The bride entwines her arm through the bend of her father's.

   The bouquet is held below the bride's waist and below the level of her father's arm so it can be seen as well as look symmetrical and graceful.

   They start down the aisle with the left foot.
- Vows should not be loud, but neither should they be inaudible.
- The bridegroom practices holding the ring so that he can slip it with ease and confidence on the bride's finger. If she is wearing long gloves, she should be able to slip her finger smoothly out of the slit of the glove.

   Also, he should be aware that it is hard for the bride to move about in a wedding dress with a train, so he should pace himself without being obvious about it.
- Remember, you are both surrounded by an affectionate company, so there is no need to feel stiff and nervous.

Have a nice life or, as the Irish say, "May the sun shine gently on your backs."

Choosing Sites for Ceremony and Reception

Q: We contracted for a reception hall and, due to a situation beyond our control, we find that the room is too large and it's too late to look for another. Besides, we'll lose the deposit. Any ideas?

The manager of the reception site can make the room look smaller by strategically placing rented screens surrounded by tall plants around the room. Even the way the buffet tables, the wedding-cake table, and bar are set up can help matters.

Ladies and Gentlemen, when selecting the house of worship and the reception site, ask how many people the premises can hold comfortably and envision your company in those premises. Most places of worship hold many more people than a reception place, but you should start with some idea of how many people are going to be invited.

If the house of worship is a considerable distance from the reception site, out-of-town guests may find it hard to locate—especially if the map directions are unclear.

Because a sense of time, place, and ambiance is often appealing to the bridal couple, it is popular now to have the ceremony and the reception in a historic mansion or town home, especially in the city of Washington and the Maryland and Virginia area. Their handsome structures are imbued with the richness of this country's beginnings. The proceeds derived from such functions are used toward upkeep and restoration.

The rooms in most manor houses are large and some have original furnishings and paintings, as do town homes though they are smaller in scale.

A historic site charges by the hour. You may have to engage a caterer from a list of caterers approved by their staff, since they know the layout and have worked there successfully. Commercial kitchens have been installed by some establishments but in others hot plates, serving pieces, place settings and cutlery, as well as tables and chairs, must be brought in by the caterer. Large catering firms have their own vans completely equipped as commercial kitchens. Other houses will allow you to bring your own food supplies, but make sure to check the kitchen facilities.

The contract might say whether or not you can have electronic music (stringed instruments are generally acceptable) and dancing. The premises must be left in good condition. Generally there is a staff overseer.

Some rooms are roped off, because during the day the mansion is a museum open to the general public and the furniture is old and fragile. This limits your access to the home. Another limiting factor is that certain sites allow receptions but not ceremonies.

In fair weather, outdoor receptions take place in the gardens of such houses, which are often extraordinarily lovely and spacious. The establishment might insist on the renting of a platform and a tent, which is necessary though an added expense.

Whether the wedding is held indoors or out, the guest list should be about the same since alternative plans must be arranged in case of rain. Rest-room facilities must be adequate for the number of people expected.

Like English gentry, some private owners of spacious houses rent in the same way that historic mansions and museums do. Apart from the above guidelines, it is advisable to check whether the owner has enough insurance coverage to handle an event such as a wedding. They should be insured against damage to *their property* and in case of a suit resulting from a business deal but also for the protection of persons renting the property.

An outdoor wedding and reception with the sky as a ceiling is considered by some a romantic setting in which to exchange marriage vows. National and state parks are available, and the expense is negligible. Again, have alternative plans in case of rain, and please, make sure rest rooms are nearby, okay?

Business catering establishments such as hotels and restaurants put everything at your fingertips. Luxury hotels offer varying package deals that sometimes include the bridal suite for use as a dressing place for the bridal party, and, if the ceremony is to take place on the premises, for the wedding night.

The catering department supplies a manager who helps guide you step by step through the proceedings during the event. They advise on the size of the banquet room for the number of guests expected, plan menu and liquor needs, and suggest an adequate serving staff.

You can use the facilities and catering of the hotel but hire other services, such as those of musicians, photographer, and florist, that are recommended to you by friends.

HOME WEDDINGS

Home weddings are successful if your house or apartment is large enough for the number of guests.

If the ceremony and reception are to take place in the house, you might have to rearrange or remove some of the furniture.

Choose an unobstructed area for the ceremony and decorate it with flowers and ribbons.

Ask the officiant for a list of items he or she will need to perform the ceremony, though most come prepared.

Guests form a semicircle, leaving an opening for the procession. It would be considerate to provide chairs for some guests who find it hard to stand for long periods of time.

Appropriate music accompanies the service, and the sound level should suit the size of the room.

Some bridal couples choose to marry in a house of worship and then return home for the reception.

If the ceremony takes place elsewhere, the bridal couple might opt for a photo session before returning to the house. In that case, someone has to be at home to greet guests and take coats.

If you are planning a garden wedding, you might have to prepare the house in case of rain or an unexpectedly cold day. A tent with a platform is a practical answer and avoids concerns about the weather and the comfort of all present.

A heavy rain during the night soaks the grass and shoes sink into the ground. It also affects musicians who need a concrete surface, especially for electronic musical instruments.

Expenses

Inquiries made by the bridegroom's family generally concern the obligations of *his* family; but the bride and her family, too, ask what are the responsibilities of *his* family. I have a sneaking suspicion that the question is the same, but not the meaning.

Traditionally, it is the bride's family who pays for the complete event with some expenses being assumed by the bridegroom's family—if they offer. After all, the bridegroom of yesteryear, no matter what his education or prospects, undertook a lifetime of responsibilities—the support and care of a wife, children, and a household. Today's woman often comes to the marriage bed with a fine education and a career equal to her husband's. In most cases she can and does support herself —she is truly an equal partner in life. If a man expects that he should not have to pay alimony to a woman who is perfectly capable of earning her own living, he should not be surprised that his participation in the cost of the wedding is expected.

But what would he say if the bride and her family want a large formal wedding and he could not see the sense in incurring such an expense? As one young man told me, "A small event with a few necessary guests and you're just as married. What is more," he continued, "I'm taking on a lifetime of responsibilities and I don't feel like blowing my hard-earned savings in one day. My wife might work, but I've seen enough of life to know that you never can tell what the future has in store. My parents are retired with an income greatly eroded over the years, and I'm not going to deplete it further. Now tell me what my obligations are and I'll meet them."

So you see, rules are difficult to set. If the bride's family wants an elaborate wedding, they will have to do it with limited help from the prospective bridegroom.

Although today more and more families share expenses, generally people with like incomes are the ones who do so, and the offer comes from his family. They both decide the type and style of the event, and expenses are split evenly—*everything*, including the rehearsal dinner.

For the young couple, whether they have a small wedding or large, there is no other time when the outlay of money will be greater in comparison to their income. The grand event aside, from that point on they will not only have to clothe themselves but also furnish a household, pay medical bills, and keep a roof over their heads. No wonder our philosophical young man had such a sense of accountability—it seems life has taught him a thing or two.

The bridegroom's expenses combine with those of his parents, since the money often comes out of one pocket, especially when the bridegroom is young. But if he is able, he and his parents might share expenses, or he may assume all costs for his side. This also applies to the bride and her family.

The suggestions below are within the general guidelines but there are groups that follow their cultural customs and those customs should be respected.

BRIDE'S AND HER FAMILY'S TRADITIONAL EXPENSES

- Invitations—including all enclosures, as well as wedding announcements
- Costs of wedding ceremony—music, fee for the house of worship, flowers, and other decorations
- Costs of entire wedding reception—music, food, wedding cake, gratuities
- Flowers carried by bride's attendants (in some areas, the bride's parents buy all flowers except the bride's going-away corsage)
- Bride's wedding dress and accessories
- Personal trousseau
- Bridegroom's wedding band for a double-ring ceremony
- Bridesmaids' gifts
- Bridesmaids' luncheon
- Engraved or printed stationery—informals and notepaper for handwritten thank-you notes and other correspondence
- Wedding-gift book
- Wedding-guest book

- Photographs, both formal and candid
- Photograph album
- Videotape recording and tapes
- Transportation for wedding party to the nuptial site, and for the bridegroom's parents and close relatives to and from the house of worship and then to the reception
- Accommodations for out-of-town members of the bride's wedding party
- Bridesmaids' luncheon

BRIDEGROOM'S AND HIS PARENTS' TRADITIONAL WEDDING EXPENSES

- Bride's engagement and wedding rings
- Marriage license
- Boutonnieres for father and male attendants
- Bride's bouquet—only if customary in your area
- Bride's going-away corsage
- Flowers for both mothers and grandmothers
- Gloves and ascots or ties for male attendants
- Wedding gift for the bride from the bridegroom—optional
- Gifts for ushers and best man
- Bachelor dinner—optional
- Officiant's fee
- Transportation for the bridal couple from the house of worship to the reception—sometimes comes within the budget of the bride's parents
- Wardrobe
- Honeymoon—unless it is given as a wedding gift
- Family's traveling expenses and hotel bill for themselves and their children
- Lodgings for out-of-town attendants, unless friends and relatives offer to put them up
- Wedding gift to the couple
- Rehearsal dinner—now customary

- Bridal album—her parents pay for the photographer and videographer, but his parents pay for the photograph *album* and *videotape*.

OPTIONAL OFFERINGS

These fall within the bridegroom's family's discretion:

- Wine, champagne, and liquor
- Music
- Flowers
- Photographer
- Videotape recording of the wedding

AN OBLIGATION:

- Any extra items requested of her family for which the bridegroom's family promised to pay.

BRIDESMAIDS' EXPENSES

- Dress, shoes, and accessories
- Travel expenses to the bride's home and back
- An individual gift for the bridal couple or a share of the attendants' joint gift
- Bridesmaids' party for the bride and bridegroom
- Shower gift—you are not expected to give more than one or two gifts, no matter how many showers you attend; or you might find small, appropriate items.
- Your lodgings are provided by the bride and her family, as are the bouquets.

BEST MAN AND USHERS

- Wedding clothes—it's nice if you own suitable formal wear, but you will need to rent it otherwise.

- Travel costs to the bridegroom's home and back
- An individual gift to the couple or a share of the "joint" present from the attendants

VARIATIONS ON A THEME

Q: What can we expect the groom's family to contribute toward wedding expenses? I'm the father of the bride. When I married, my family undertook certain obligations even though the bride's side didn't approach us. We just said we would help. My wife called the bridegroom's parents to ask point blank what they intended to contribute to the affair. Their answer was that they'll show up.

I don't know how you can pry an offer from them. The only option you have to keep expenses down is to limit the guest list. I am not advising or advocating this, but I've known people to limit the bridegroom's guest list drastically so that if his family needed extra invitations, it would be at their expense.

Q: Naw. It's my daughter's wedding, and I want her to be happy.

Ladies and Gentlemen, it is important that a meeting take place between parents right after their children decide to marry. In this case we have to ask: Did her family discuss wedding plans with his family in the beginning and give them an opening to express their opinion? If they had, that would have given both families an opportunity for frank discussion. Did they tell his family that it is going to be a formal wedding, with an open bar, a seated dinner with dancing, and that they can invite a certain number with no leeway for extras—even though his family might have expressed a willingness to pay for the overflow?

That can lead to a sensitive and painful situation for the families. However, if you ask the couple on their honeymoon how they felt about the wedding, they will say it was all worth it.

PROMISE 'EM ANYTHING

Q: *My daughter's in-laws promised to contribute to certain extras that we had no intention of including for the wedding. Well, I paid for everything, thinking that when I sent them their share of the bill that a check would be forthcoming. So far we haven't received a penny, though months have gone by. How do I handle such a touchy subject?*

Send your son-in-law's parents itemized photocopies of bills you incurred on their behalf and for which they had assumed responsibility.

Had you spoken to me before the wedding, when they originally suggested the extras, I would have advised that the bride-groom's parents deal with the tradespeople themselves. That approach is more tactful and avoids embarrassment. If you'd felt my suggestion crass, I'd have said that there will be a much better relationship with your daughter's in-laws in the future. Now you have feelings of resentment and of being taken advantage of.

CHAMPAGNE PROMISES

The bride's family was paying for the wedding and reception. The reception included an open bar and wine at a sit-down dinner. However, for the toast, champagne would be served only to those at the bridal table; the rest of the guests would have wine, which is an acceptable practice.

No, no, sang the generous father of the bridegroom; everyone will have extra-fine champagne at his expense—just send the bill to him. After the wedding, her family sent him the bill, but he did not keep his promise.

Clothing—
Attendants—
Parties

Clothing

When the bride wears a formal bridal gown that has a long train and a headdress holding the bridal veil, the bridegroom wears formal dress to complement her. The bridal ensemble determines what everyone else wears.

Lucky is the bride for whom the "something old" is going to be an heirloom wedding dress handed down from one generation to the other.

If "something new" is going to be the dress you wear on your wedding day, start the search early—six months ahead—because so much depends on delivery and finding accessories. You might choose white, but there are varying hues of white such as écru, eggshell, or a pale tint of your favorite color. Some brides set their hearts on bolder colors.

You might be enamored of the first frock in the first store, but it is likely to take more of an effort than that.

Attend the bridal shows that are so popular now. January, February, and March are bridal-show months but, since they attract the public, some firms show the next season's fashions in August. Magazines are excellent sources for what styles are fashionable.

Keep in mind that the bridal gown is the most expensive part of the regalia and that the total outlay has to include the veil and accessories.

You might be good to your pocketbook by tracking when wedding dresses go on sale, but shop only in stores that stand behind their merchandise. There are two major concerns when buying a dress on sale: The material has to be compatible with the time of year the wedding is to take place, and the garment must be in good condition. If it looks slightly shopworn, but you love it and the price is right, ask the salesperson if it is restorable. If she or you have doubts, forget it. However, if all it needs is a cleaning by a store that specializes in wedding gowns, buy the dress with the stipulation that it could be returned if the cleaners feel it will look too faded. Have the salesperson write the proviso on the sales receipt as proof of the agreement.

Some brides found their dresses through a newspaper's classified advertising section—dresses that were new! However, it has to be a perfect fit, or else you will have to visit a competent dressmaker.

In a recently published book, the writer railed against charges for alterations on wedding gowns; that impels me to offer an explanation to brides.

When you choose a gown from a retail shop, your measurements are taken and the order is sent to the manufacturer. The real fitting begins when the gown comes in from the manufacturer, who will send your size but not to your exact measurements. The store's seamstress does the alterations. As with any ready-made garment that needs alteration bought from any retail store, there are charges. A perfect fit is a perfect look.

If you wish a *custom-made* wedding gown, a dressmaker is what you need. Be sure to look at his or her work and ask for *references*. You choose the material and style and make changes in the design—sleeves from one pattern, a modified neckline, et cetera. The material and the style should complement each other. The dressmaker takes your measurements and gradually, after a few fittings, the dress is ready—the charge includes all services.

Stores have varying policies regarding the purchase of wedding gowns. Know the ground rules of the establishment before signing on the dotted line and handing over the deposit, which is legally binding. The store may have a limited cancellation period—in some cases, only five days from the date of the receipt, after which you have made a commitment.

The delivery date is noted on the deposit receipt. To avoid a harrowing last-minute experience, some brides request delivery three weeks earlier than the actual date of the wedding. But do not do so if your weight fluctuates.

The length of the train is measured from the floor out. The sweep length is half a foot, the chapel length is almost two feet, and the elegant cathedral length over two feet. Some gowns have a detachable train that is removed for the reception.

As with everything to do with *informal* weddings, clothing is not only a simpler choice but more practical—an afternoon dress or suit with matching shoes, and a hat. A small nosegay cluster or a pinned-on corsage completes the outfit.

Those are general guidelines, but there is no guarantee what will be in style during the next year or so. Men's styles, on the other hand, seem constant.

After six, the ceremony is considered an evening wedding.

The *very formal daytime or evening* wedding in a large house of worship lends itself to the cathedral-length train and a long veil.

Looking in the mirror, ask yourself whether the dress wears you or you wear it. Wear your wedding shoes during trying-on sessions at the store. If the back of the dress is cut low, the store might suggest sewing bra cups to the underbodice.

Sleeves may be long or short depending on the time of year. There may be an objection to bare arms and shoulders in a house of worship. Speak to the officiant about whether elbow-length gloves are required; they are worn at evening weddings.

The veil may be sweep, chapel, or cathedral length. A separate face veil is attached to the headpiece and carefully lifted over the cap during the ceremony and removed at the reception. Try the headpiece on before a three-way mirror, viewing it from all angles. You might think a Juliet cap suits you best until you try on the mantilla.

Semiformal daytime and evening dresses are floor length—with or without a short train; the veil is short. For other lengths—ankle, princess (which is a mite above the ankle), ballerina, or cocktail—the veil should suit the outfit.

Silk suits or cocktail- or street-length dresses are suitable for *informal daytime.*

For *informal evening* weddings, long gowns or cocktail or afternoon frocks are the choices.

ENTER THE BRIDEGROOM

Your lady has chosen her regalia. Now you, sir, and the male members of the wedding party dress according to the time of day, the time of year, and the formality of your bride's apparel.

Men seem to have gone back to the traditional styles, at least in the Washington, D.C., area.

For a *daytime* wedding, the cutaway is the *traditional* formal attire for the bridegroom and his entourage. Try it on, you might like it.

A tuxedo is suitable evening formal wear all year around after six o'clock. It is practical to buy one for future formal occasions, because tuxedos do not go out of style.

Whether renting or buying, you and your groomsmen need to choose your outfits at least two months before the wedding.

Now for the traditional . . .
- *Very formal daytime:* Black or gray cutaway coat, striped gray trousers, gray waistcoat, winged-collar shirt, ascot or striped tie, and plain black shoes and socks.
- *Very formal evening:* White tie, black tail coat, matching satin-striped trousers, white waistcoat, studded stiff front-winged collar shirt with cuff-linked French cuffs, black socks, and black patent-leather or kid shoes.
- *Formal/semiformal daytime:* Black or charcoal gray sack coat or stroller, waistcoat, striped trousers, turned-down-collar

dress shirt with French cuffs, black-and-gray-striped tie, and black socks and shoes.

- *Formal/semiformal evening:* Black tuxedo, white dress shirt with turned-down collar and French cuffs, black vest or cummerbund, black bow tie, black shoes. Summer: white dinner jacket and cummerbund.
- *Informal day and evening:* Dark blue or dark gray suit, white soft shirt, striped tie, black socks and oxfords.
- The bridegroom and the best man dress alike but have different-colored boutonnieres.

HERE COME THE BRIDESMAIDS

Honor attendants and bridesmaids wear long dresses with shoes dyed to match and have short veils or flowered head-dresses that match the colors in the bouquet.

Gloves go well with short sleeves.

The bride may want all the attendants to wear the same color and style dresses, or she may wish that the bridesmaids and matron of honor look slightly different.

At less-formal weddings, maid and matron of honor wear pretty afternoon frocks, long or short, as the bride wishes, and shoes dyed to match. They carry small bouquets.

At an *informal* wedding they wear dresses and flowers to go with the bride's outfit.

Junior bridesmaids' bouquets, headwear, and dresses conform in style and color to those of the older bridesmaids, though they are less sophisticated. Slippers should be a height suitable to the wearers' ages. They wear gloves if the brides-maids do.

Junior ushers wear the same formal wear as the ushers.

Flower girls dress in a manner suited to their ages. They wear ribbons or flowered wreaths in their hair and carry baskets—with or without petals in them.

Ring bearers are clad in navy blue suits, knee-high navy blue socks and black shoes. Train bearers wear white suits, white knee socks, and white shoes and, if very young, velvet suits.

MOTHERS' CLOTHING

Very formal daytime and evening: Mothers wear long or cocktail-length dresses, with shoes dyed to match. Headwear is chosen to suit the costume and gloves. Flowers can be wrist corsages.

Formal/semiformal day or evening: Long, cocktail- or street-length frocks. At the moment, hats are in style.

Informal day or evening: Mothers wear silk suits or cocktail dresses.

SECOND WEDDING

Until recently, etiquette dictated that women marrying for the second time dressed simply. Conservative brides still follow those guidelines. A pastel suit or a silk afternoon dress are suitable.

There is an abundance of materials to choose from—the almost bridey-looking to soft silk, moiré, linen, and faille as well as the newer synthetics that look much like the natural cloths. Headdresses follow the same mode.

The bride wants to achieve the look of a bride, but not to duplicate the first time she was married in her early twenties. She asks herself the same questions when choosing a bridal outfit as she does when she chooses any article of clothing— Is it suitable for the occasion and does it fit? Most follow that pattern in varying degrees.

Young women wear a bridal gown but no veil. The headdress might be white seed pearls entwined in a pouf netting or a flowered arrangement that rests gracefully toward the back of the head. She might hold a bouquet or an arrangement of fresh long-stemmed flowers.

Some second-time brides reason that a wedding dress is

uniquely a bride's outfit and may be worn by a bride even though she has been married before.

HAPPY BUT RELUCTANT DRESSER

Q: *The bridegroom's father gleefully refuses to wear formal clothing, saying that he isn't in the wedding party and doesn't have to stand in the receiving line. Please say he's wrong!*

He's right and, yet, he's sort of wrong. What I mean is that in a Christian wedding, the bridegroom's father is not involved in the ceremony, unless he serves as the bridegroom's best man or is asked to be in the receiving line. If he has no function other than circulating among the guests, then he can wear the same attire as the guests—except that he wears a boutonniere.

However, fathers should dress in formal clothes if the bride would like to achieve a unified look, especially if it is a white- or a black-tie affair.

RING BEARER'S TEMPEST

Q: *My husband's twenty-one-year-old sister is being married. She asked my five-year-old to be the ring bearer, but when I heard she wanted him to wear a tuxedo, I said that's ridiculous—he'll wear an Eton suit or nothing. She said nothing it was. I became angry and told her I wouldn't come to the wedding. My husband is very angry with me and wants me to apologize. Am I so wrong?*

Wait a minute! Are you really not going to the wedding? Picture a teapot and try to create a tempest in it . . . that is what you are doing. If you can't meet her requirements, then okay, your little one won't be the ring bearer, but saying you aren't going to the wedding is involving not only your husband but his entire family. You're chancing a split of long duration —and over the outfit of a five-year-old! You may not agree with the bride's taste or decision, but she does have a right to state what she wishes those in her bridal party to wear. Calm down and do the sporting thing; telephone and say you over-reacted. The only person allowed to have nervous palpitations is the bride.

LONG ENOUGH TO REACH THE GROUND

Q: My stepdaughter is being married. Both the bridegroom's mother and I would like to wear street-length dresses, but the bride tells me her mother is wearing long. Why can't we wear what we want?

You can wear whatever length you wish, unless you and the bride's father are hosts; then you would want to wear full-length. However, the bridegroom's mother is next to the last to be seated at church, and she stands in the receiving line at the reception. That's why mothers wear the same-length dress.

DE GUSTIBUS NON EST DISPUTANDUM

Q: You'll think this is a minor problem, but I'm in a temper. As mother of the bridegroom I picked an expensive and perfectly appropriate dress to wear to the wedding. When my future daughter-in-law and her mother saw it, they expressed displeasure. Then, when I saw her wedding gown, the maids' dresses, and what her mother was going to wear, I knew why. I've never seen outfits so tacky-looking and never have I had a dress like theirs on my back—styleless, formless, eighty-dollar dresses that hang loosely on the body. Do you remember the comic strip "Li'l Abner," whose wedding was the two-dollar kind? I'm astounded by my son, who tells me I'm trying to outshine the bride and I should wear something that goes with their "taste." What should I do? Do I wear what I bought or buy a dress in which I will feel ashamed? My family will wonder what came over me. What are the ground rules?

As translated from Latin: Where taste is concerned, there is no arguing. The ground rules are that the mother of the bridegroom follows the color scheme and length set by the bride. Her family has no right to dictate the quality of the choice. To suggest that you look for another dress doesn't seem to be the solution since, obviously, your taste is so different from theirs. I'm tempted to say go with what you've chosen and worry only about your son's reaction—it's a dilemma.

Ladies and Gentlemen, after the wedding Mrs. In-Law called to place the wedding announcement. She *rented* a mother-of-the-bridegroom dress in an appropriate length and shade for *forty dollars and change*—the bridal rental shop even altered it to fit. However, because she did not want future generations to see her so adorned, she stood sideways during the photo session with the bride and bridegroom, and the table-hopping shots showed her head perched between two people. She said her son had no reason to complain.

Good show! Mrs. In-Law has won my undying admiration for her sportsmanship.

> *Will you wear white, oh, my dear, oh, my dear*
> *Oh, will you wear white, charming guest?*
> *No, I won't wear white, 'cause the bride will have my life,*
> *Oh, I will buy me . . . Ah, you'll have to wait and see*
> *Oh, will you wear black, oh, my dear, oh, my dear*
> *Oh, will you wear black, charming guest?*
> *No, I won't wear black 'cause you'll be on my back,*
> *Oh, I'll buy me . . . Ah, why don't you wait and see*
> *But, will you wear gray, oh, my future ma-in-law?*
> *Oh, will you wear gray, charming lady?*
> *Gray? Gray? In that you have no say.*

My dear, I've bought me a dress!

COLOR PERCEPTION

A word about color perception.

Although some wedding guests will try to avoid wearing either black or white to a wedding, there are those who think that is rubbish. They don't wear bridal white, and in no way do their ensembles resemble that of a bride.

I have attended bridal shows featuring "snowball" weddings—the *entire* bridal party was clad in white, male and female. Fathers of the bride wore the traditional outfit for a white- or black-tie affair.

The next breaking of the color-scheme barrier is the wearing of black for the bridesmaids.

Young people today do not associate black with sadness, though at one time, women in mourning wore black for a year and men wore black armbands around the upper left sleeve of their jackets. A woman in mourning was allowed to wear variations of mauve at family functions such as weddings, and when spending the summer in the country she wore white from head to toe. In the East, women wear white for the same reason but gown themselves in orange-red for celebrations.

In the past, red was verboten as being too bold, and no nice girl wore it. Remember the impetuous Jezebel? She did not get away with her choice of color and paid the price.

GARB-GUESSING GUEST

Q: *My sister's daughter is being married this summer. Do you think my sons may go to church in shirtsleeves? Since they're growing so fast and will get so little wear from them, I am reluctant to buy them jackets.*

I think it is appropriate for them to have jackets on during the ceremony, even though the attire of little children not in the bridal party might go unnoticed. By the way, how old are they?

Q: *Thirteen and fifteen.*

Please! I thought from the way you were talking about them, that they are little ones. It would be inappropriate for two young men to go to church and to their cousin's wedding in shirtsleeves.

Q: *Oh, I was hoping I could tell my sister that Mrs. Gruen said it would be all right and that would be that.*

Mrs. Gruen says that's not fair!

Q: *(Laughter) I know.*

Ladies and Gentlemen, one has to know the right questions to ask!

GUESTS' CLOTHING

The guests wear attire suited to the time of day and the formality of the occasion. Daytime attire is generally street dresses or suits—the length is according to the current mode. Next year, who knows? If hats are worn, gloves are also.

I have worn hats to church weddings and was the only woman in the company that had one on. Gloves seem to be worn only during winter weather.

Below is the traditional dress code . . .

• *Very formal daytime:* cocktail or smart street-length dresses; hats and gloves are appropriate. Men: dark business suits.
• *Very formal evening:* long or cocktail dresses. Men: tuxedos.

- *Formal/semiformal daytime:* cocktail dresses or short dresses. Men: dark suits.
- *Informal daytime:* street-length dresses. Gloves and hats for the house of worship.
- *Formal evening* after six o'clock: If his lady wears a long dress, then he wears a tuxedo. If she has a cocktail dress, then he wears a business suit.
- *Informal/semiformal daytime:* street-length dresses.

Sometimes the formality of dress depends on the part of the country the wedding takes place in. If you live in the South where evening weddings are more formal, and the wedding is up North, telephone the bride's family to ask what attire is customary for that area. If you do not fancy being so direct, call that town's department store or a hotel there for advice.

Attendants

A friend may well be reckoned the masterpiece of nature.
—Emerson

Should the bride and bridegroom have such friends as Emerson describes, they will try to find ways of bringing them into the wedding party. However, should the couple be unable to give them any special honors, Emersonian friends will understand. If there are many close young relatives and the wedding is small, it may be that only family members will participate. Sensitivity will be the most important asset on which the betrothed, relatives, and friends will have to rely.

Traditionally, the bride and bridegroom choose brothers and sisters as attendants, and they also try to include each other's siblings. After all, who but siblings have known the bridal couple all their lives, and are not most weddings family affairs?

Of course, it all depends on what has happened within the

family structure way before a new person comes into its fold.

One of the fascinating things about the Washington, D.C., area is that conglomerates of people who live there were born elsewhere in the United States, not to mention overseas. I have spoken to many about choosing wedding-party members. Though the general practice and published advice, center on siblings, for some regional areas there is no set pattern and the final decision depends largely on cultural customs.

It might be customary that the bridegroom's side chooses family before friends but that the bride's custom is to ask friends, even though there are brothers and sisters in both families.

Think carefully before choosing an attendant; the person should be more than an acquaintance because there is time and expense involved (see Expenses.)

Apart from the affection of the family circle, the practical aspect of asking family members into the bridal party is that they have expenses and an obligation to the bride and bridegroom anyway.

The number of attendants waiting on both the bride and bridegroom depends on the size of the wedding.

An ultraformal wedding held in a large place of worship has up to twelve bridesmaids, including the flower girl and junior bridesmaids, and twelve groomsmen, including the ring bearer. Less-formal affairs generally have from one to six. There should be one usher for every fifty guests. The number of maids depends on the wishes of the bride. There may be a need for more ushers than maids.

The role of attendant carries a commitment—a promise to the bride and bridegroom. They should be wholeheartedly part of the prenuptial events, on time for the rehearsal, and be at the ceremony site at the designated time.

The bride selects her maid of honor from those who are young and have never been married. The matron of honor should be a married woman, a divorcée, or a widow. The maid of honor takes precedence over the matron of honor, even if both are equally related to the bride or equally close as friends.

HIS SISTER, HER BROTHERS

Q: My daughter has asked two close friends to be matron and maid of honor, respectively. Her fiancé invited his closest friend to be best man and his sister's husband, who is also a business associate, to be the usher. I think her future sister-in-law will feel left out.

Your daughter doesn't have to invite more attendants than she wishes. It won't be a balanced grouping if she decides to invite his sister, but including her might cement the relationship. If invited, the bridesmaid and the usher could stand together during the ceremony.

Ladies and Gentlemen, when wedding plans begin, the bridal couple state the terms but soon find they do not stand alone. Those shadowy figures in the other's family, and suddenly in their own as well, start a prenuptial dance known as protocol and etiquette.

HOW YOUNG IS YOUNG?

Q: My only sister is twelve years old. Since our mother died we have been very close, and now that I am being married her life is being disrupted again. I would like her to be my maid of honor and only attendant. I've mentioned it confidentially to a few people and they have never heard of someone so young performing those duties. Have you?

You're the bride and the choice is yours. Go ahead with your plans if you think that your sister is mature enough, and, I venture to say, she must be, given the loss she has suffered.

Twelve-year-old girls are quite grown up and sensible. She can be your maid of honor. Have more than one private rehearsal with her.

QUID PRO QUO

Q: I was maid of honor for my best friend, who has no sisters. Now that I am being married, she expects me to ask her to be the matron of honor, but I have a married sister. I don't want to hurt my friend, but what can I do?

I think your friend will understand when you explain. If possible, invite her to be a bridesmaid.

Q: Can a married woman be a bridesmaid?

Of course.

Yes, Ladies and Gentlemen, allow me to quickly explain that I do know that the origin of maids in the rock-throwing stage of man was to provide a virginal circle around the bride, and to help her dress and prepare for the loss of maidenhood in our not-too-distant past. But, please, nowadays? Diogenes, whose ancient quest was to find an honest man, had it easy. . . .

MY HOSTESS, MY MATRON OF HONOR?

Q: My daughter has asked me to be her matron of honor. It is her way of showing love and saying that I am special to her. However, I feel a little uneasy and am wondering if it's really the proper thing to do.

Think carefully about being the matron of honor, even if you feel you can handle it with all you have to do. The bride's mother has the most important and taxing role to perform as the eyes and ears of every facet of the event. Also, once your husband has escorted the bride to the altar, you will not be sitting next to him in the first pew watching the exchange of vows.

A friend of mine, whose daughter's wedding was a great success, told me she has one lingering regret. She was so involved in looking after a houseful of guests on the wedding day that by the time she was able to rush upstairs to help her daughter dress, the process was over; there stood the bride looking absolutely lovely in her formal attire. It did not dawn on her until the wedding was over and her daughter had left for her honeymoon that she had let that special time between mother and daughter slip by her.

IS THE MAID OF HONOR THE BEST MAN?

Ladies and Gentlemen, with the permission of my daughter-in-law, Ruth, below is a repeat of conversations held when she and my son were in the stages of planning a small wedding. They were married in 1983. First I will set the scene.

Ruth has a small family whom she loves dearly—just her mother, father, and brother.

"Mom," she said, "I'm thinking of asking my brother, Steve, to be my only attendant. What do you think?"

"That's a fine idea," I answered.

Ruth on the phone to Steven: "Steve, I've a great idea. I would like you to be my maid of honor."

Steve: "You've got to be kidding!"

A day or two later Ruth telephones Steve again.

Ruth: "Steve, I've got a great idea!"

Steve: "I can't possibly be your handmaiden."

Ruth: "Look. Richard's brother, Mark, is going to be his best man. There's no reason you can't be my best man. You could both walk down the aisle together."

Steve: "Now you're talking."
It was a lovely wedding.

In the past, having male members of the bridal party serving the bride and females serving the bridegroom was unheard of —but not any longer.

And now to the invaluable services of the best man . . .

BEST MAN AND USHERS

Since the best man is the one closest to the bridegroom, his role is to anticipate the events and take an active part. His responsibilities include overseeing the ushers. If the wedding is a large one, he and the bridegroom designate a head usher— preferably a family member who knows many of the guests.

LIST FOR BEST MAN AND USHERS
- Rent the appropriate outfits.
- Appear on time for fittings.
- Give bridegroom the glove sizes of his entourage.
- Make every effort to attend prewedding parties.
- Discuss suggestions for the joint wedding present.
- Be on time for wedding rehearsal.
- Punctuality is essential on the wedding day; arrive at the house of worship at the designated time.
- Seat guests before the wedding ceremony starts.
- Participate in the ceremony.
- Assist in all phases of the day.

On the wedding day, the best man arrives early at the bridegroom's home with a checklist of reminders to prevent any last-minute hitches. He sees to it that the bridegroom is organized and appropriately attired. One by one, he goes over the checklist:

- Marriage license
- Ring
- Checkbook, charge cards, ready money; driver's license, car keys, as well as a tank of gasoline
- Passport and travel tickets, if the couple is going abroad
- Hotel reservations
- Luggage for the wedding trip and the overnight bag
- Best man puts the envelope with fee and the bridegroom's note of thanks for clergyman in his inside jacket pocket.
- Transporting arrangements for the bride and bridegroom after the ceremony to the reception
- A few taxicab telephone numbers in the event of an emergency
- Return the bridegroom's rented suit to the shop, if his parents live out of town and are leaving the next day

The best man and the bridegroom arrive at the house of worship at least twenty minutes before the ceremony. Both wait in the vestry until it is time to walk together to the chancel. The best man holds the ring in his vest pocket or on his own finger until it is time to hand it to the clergyman, and he acts as witness and signs the marriage certificate.

In a Jewish wedding, a relative by blood or marriage cannot act as a witness even if he performs the duties of best man.

Traditionally, the best man will propose the first toast to the newly married couple at the reception and, if the family wishes, read the telegrams and Mailgrams.

When the family stands in the receiving line, he is expected to mix with the company.

The best man needs to know, among other things, if there will be a photo session directly after the ceremony and how the bride and bridegroom will be transported after the ceremony. He might be needed to drive the couple to the reception and later to the airport or train station.

USHERS

The usher stands to the left of the portal and greets guests as they arrive. He asks which side of the family they know, extends his right arm to the lady and, with the gentleman walking a step or two behind, escorts her to the correct pew. Some couples prefer to walk together rather than be conducted by this formal method, but the usher still leads the way.

When the wedding is extremely large, there may be more reserved pews than the first two that seat close family. Guests hand a pew card to the usher, and he leads them to the designated pew. Two ushers lay down the canvas runner, which may be white paper instead of canvas.

Ushers should participate in the festivities and are participants in the processional and recessional. Ushers do not stand in the receiving line. At the reception, they dance, dance, dance, and are eager to catch the garter. Okay, fellas. I quit.

MAID/MATRON OF HONOR

The honor attendant makes herself available to the bride as much as she can. There are so many ways before the actual wedding day to be of help, perhaps by addressing wedding invitations or organizing the bride's list and index cards; and, if needed, she may help with arranging the seating for the reception—a last-minute chore.

As with the best man, the honor attendant knows what the procedures will be so that, on her part, the wedding ceremony will go well. She also needs to know time and transportation schedules.

- The maid of honor prepares a list of what is needed on the wedding day and checks items off as they are accomplished.

- She organizes the bridesmaids and together they discuss entertaining the bride.
- She reminds the bridesmaids when to go for dress fittings.
- She and the bridesmaids attend the rehearsal and the function that takes place before or after it.
- On the wedding day, she calmly assists the bride.
- The honor attendant should dress before the bride so she can be helpful to her and her mother.

The honor attendant arrives at the house of worship at least at the designated time.

In a double-ring ceremony, the honor attendant holds the bridegroom's ring. However, if there is a ring bearer, the honor attendant lifts the ring off the cushion, which is secured by a thread to hold the ring in place and is easy to remove. (One little three-year-old did not want to relinquish the ring or the cushion. "It's mine," he told everyone, much to the amusement of all present.)

During the processional, she immediately precedes the bride.

Her main responsibility to the bride during the ceremony is to straighten the train, hold the bride's flowers, see to her veil, and produce the bridegroom's ring. For the recessional, she straightens the bride's train as the bride turns to face the congregation, returns her bouquet, and most of all, is alert to the bride's needs during the proceedings.

At the rehearsal, she knows on which side of the bride she is to stand during the ceremony, whether she will be the one to keep an eye on the flower girl, and when to walk with the best man during the recessional.

She stands in the receiving line, unless it is a short one, sits at the bridal table, joins in the festivities and, if necessary, signs the marriage certificate.

Sometimes the bridal couple stay until the reception is over, but if they need to leave for their wedding trip beforehand, then the honor attendant assists the bride as she puts on her going-away costume. If need be, she takes care of the bridal gown and veil.

BRIDESMAIDS

The bride, when she invites her relatives or friends to attend her, is saying that they are special to her. They, in turn, form a warm circle of friendship around the bride by cooperating as much as they can. Their responsibilities to her are not as demanding as those of the maid of honor, but they should try to be of help to both.

If possible, bridesmaids give a party for the bride and take that opportunity to give a joint wedding present. The bride, in turn, honors them with some sort of function and gives them presents of appreciation for their support of her.

Gracefully, the bridesmaids walk down the aisle, completing the circle of friendship for the bride.

Prewedding Parties

It is exciting, whatever one's age, to attend the round of parties that serve to introduce one to the other's friends. However, the exhilarating whirl combined with preparations for the wedding is sometimes responsible for that ring-around-the-eyes look so deftly touched up by clever photographers in pictures for the newspaper. Try to combine some of the parties.

Now, on to the celebrations . . .

REHEARSAL DINNER

Anyone may offer to entertain other than the bridegroom and his parents: the bride's parents, a member of the clan on either side, or a good friend who wants to entertain for the family.

To be sporting about it—if the bride's parents are footing the cost of the entire wedding, it is a gracious way for the bridegroom's family to assume a part of the expenses by hosting the rehearsal dinner. If the wedding is a joint venture, then the rehearsal dinner—as with the rest of the arrangements—is discussed and costs included in the expenses.

The rehearsal dinner is one of the most enjoyable of all prenuptial gatherings because it brings together the bridal party, guests from out of town, and close family members. After initial welcoming words from the host, he or she toasts the bridal couple and includes welcoming remarks about the person his or her child is marrying. The bride's father or mother then returns the compliment. After the meal is over, the best man raises his glass in tribute to the bridegroom and says kind words to the bride; others follow. It is an intimate time with good-natured ribbing and happy laughter.

Q: I expect to marry in a few weeks. My parents are hosting the rehearsal dinner, intending to invite only those in the bridal party and immediate family members. My bride's parents want us to invite those coming to the wedding from out of town, but my parents are reluctant and say they don't have to do so. Are they right?

They are right; they do not have to invite out-of-town guests, but it is a gracious thing to do and creates goodwill. Sometimes, the bride's parents offer to contribute to expenses that are incurred in the rehearsal festivities.

There isn't much else I can say other than suggest to your parents that they give a simple buffet supper of cold meats, salads, assorted breads, cheeses, hot and cold drinks, little cakes and cookies, and wine or champagne to toast the couple.

Q: Do we have to invite both clergymen to the rehearsal dinner? We are having two officiants, one of whom we do not know.

Does the clergyman know the people who invited him to officiate?

Q: *Yes, he's the bridegroom's minister.*

Then both are invited.

Ladies and Gentlemen, the rehearsal-dinner invitation should request a response, especially if it takes place in a restaurant or a rented place.

Some attendants and out-of-town guests may be unable to arrive on time.

If it is a very small gathering, invite people by telephone or send handwritten notes. If the guest list is large, it might be a time-saver to have them printed, or use the popular at-home cards. Above your name, write:

> *Rehearsal dinner for Jill and Frederick*
> *YOUR NAMES*
> *Thursday, May 28, at 6 o'clock*
> *The Montpelier*
> *Concord, Mass.*

Please reply
(Telephone number)

If you wish, add your address along with your telephone number.

Handwritten notes on blank informals are also fine:

> Dear Mrs. Herman [or use her given name],
> Harold and I do hope you and John are able to attend the dinner we are planning for Jill and Frederick after the wedding rehearsal.
> Our house on Thursday, May 28, at 7:30 p.m. Please phone or write whether you can come.
>
> > Sincerely [*or* Affectionately],
> > Sarah Hampenstance

- The rehearsal dinner may be hosted by anyone who feels like doing it, but it is usually given by the bridegroom's parents.
- The hosts decide whether to have a buffet meal in a private home or a seated dinner at a club.
- Rehearsal-dinner invitations are mailed about two weeks before the wedding *and after acceptances have been received.*
  They are not included with the wedding invitations, since those who sponsor the wedding might not necessarily be the same people hosting the rehearsal dinner.
- Invitations are phoned, handwritten, or engraved, depending on the formality of the party planned.
- The entire wedding party and fiancé(e)s, but not casual dates, are invited—sometimes including the clergypersons and spouses, if they are friends. Also included are the younger attendants, if they can take the excitement, along with their parents.
- At a home function, seating might be arranged, but sometimes there is a lack of space. No matter what, the bride and bridegroom sit next to each other.
- At a more formal function the best man sits on the bride's right and the maid or matron of honor on the bridegroom's left. The bride's mother sits to the right of the host at one end of the table. The hostess sits at the other end with the bride's father on her right.
- The first toast is a welcoming one by the host.

HAVE YOU HEARD OF AN INFARE?

It was an American custom in the 1880s. In those days, when the bride's parents hosted the wedding-day feast, the bridegroom's parents gave an infare the following day that was essentially another feast.

Now the equivalent is a Sunday-morning breakfast designed to send guests on the road home with warm feelings toward their hospitable hosts. The menu consists of eggs, fresh fruits, rolls and butter, coffee, tea, orange juice, and small Danish pastries and whatever else the host or hostess wishes to serve. The bridal couple may be able to attend if they are still in town. It is a relaxed time. The company exchanges recollections of the previous day—conversations one would not be privy to otherwise.

BRIDAL SHOWERS

A book written in the 1920s waxes condescending about showers but admits that they are "kindly meant."

Though so many etiquette books were written for city or town people, country people and various ethnic groups in this country held to the practice and now showers are accepted and enjoyed by everyone.

The bridal shower originated in Europe. The peasant bride went from house to house inviting each dweller to her wedding. They, in turn, gave the bride items from their household.

Now it is a gathering of intimate people who bring gifts to help the young bride gather "little" items for her household and her trousseau. However, those sponsoring a bridal shower assume its cost. Sending out an invitation soliciting financial help from potential guests is simply not done—unless *everybody* jointly decides to host the shower. Guests, with the exception of the bride-elect, should know the ground rules.

If the bride does not want a shower and you are sure she means it, the wish is honored. She may just be embarrassed, so speak to Mother. Mother, please be direct in your answer. If she is firm about it, and you still want to entertain for her, have a tea or a luncheon that does not require presents from those attending.

I understand that some people give the wedding present at the time of the shower, but I am not advocating the idea.

SHOWER GUIDELINES

- Immediate family members on either side—parents, sisters, brothers—do not host bridal showers. To do so would give the appearance of asking for presents.
- Aunts, cousins, neighbors, and friends may host showers.
- It is customary for the maid or matron of honor and the bridesmaids, if they are not immediate family, to give a joint shower the week of the wedding.
- When the bride is alone and has only a few friends, a member of the bridegroom's family takes matters in hand by enlisting a trusted outsider to host the event—even though the family assumes the expense. Discretion, please.
- Both mothers are invited to showers that concentrate on family and should try to attend; they take gifts.
- Fellow workers sometimes surprise the bride. For such showers, invitations are limited to those at work.
- Invitations are not sent to people living a long distance away; they will probably not be able to attend but will feel obligated to send a gift.
- There is no obligation to send a present if you cannot attend a shower. The only exceptions would be the bridegroom's mother, grandmothers, or godmothers and close family who might want to send presents instead of being there in person.
- Combined gifts may be given, but the idea of a shower is to unwrap pretty packages and comment on the originality of the purchases, all the while adding a few oohs and aahs.
- Showers take place any time *after the wedding invitations have been sent,* and only those invited to all events associated with the wedding receive shower invitations.
- Guests should arrive on schedule, since most showers are supposed to be a surprise to the bride. Often, however, a surprise party is not practical because of the busy schedule of today's bride and hosts.
- Both men and women can participate.

• Some showers have a theme, or the party can be a "bring-whatever-you-wish shower."

THEME IDEAS
• *Alphabet:* Each guest is assigned a letter of the alphabet that is listed on the invitation. Guests choose a gift starting with that letter. It guarantees a variety.
• *For an avid sports-playing bride and bridegroom:* Tennis accessories are always welcome. Golf accessories such as clickers (score-keeping tool) or beads on a string (an abacus) are useful.
• *Memorabilia:* Mostly for an intimate gathering of family and the closest of friends. Gifts are whimsical—tug-at-memories kind. Guests bring something tangible that has to do with the past: for example, Grandmother's framed embroidered winter scene that she worked on many an evening or Grandfather's shaving mug now holding a fresh plant.
• *Cup-and-saucer collection:* It is an old fashioned idea. Each guest brings a decorative cup and saucer, and the bride now has an assortment for cake-and-coffee occasions.
• *Gourmet accessories for the bride who loves to cook:* A dish with the giver's recipe is a perennial favorite. The dish may be a casserole; write your favorite recipe on an index-sized card.
• *Garden tools:* "How-to" books on gardening, or a variety of fresh herbs for the bride and bridegroom, are a good idea.

Some detective work at the bridal registry will garner ideas. On the invitation the hostess suggests the color schemes for bathroom items, bed linen, blankets (check sizes), and kitchen towels.

• Shower gifts need not be expensive.
• Notify by telephone, handwritten notes, or printed shower

cards that indicate the time, date, location, and whether it is to be a tea, luncheon, or cocktail party. Don't forget to ask for a response by telephone.

- Presents, along with a note from the giver, are brought to the party and placed around the bridal chair, which has an opened lace-edged white umbrella attached to it.

- The host decides when presents are opened; generally it takes place before the refreshments are served.

- Seated in the bridal chair, the bride-to-be opens each present as the honor attendant reads the accompanying card aloud. Meanwhile, someone keeps the cards and gifts together and notes the item and giver so that the bride has a record.

- A bouquet, from the ribbons and bows that wrapped each gift, is made by cutting slits in a strong paper plate and inserting the ribbons so that they hang loosely. Stuck on top are bows in assorted sizes and colors. It makes a charming centerpiece on the buffet table afterward. And just for fun, the bride may want to wear it on her head at the luncheon and at the rehearsal dinner.

- Playing games and winning small prizes can be fun at a shower. One popular game is a Scrabble one using wedding clues.

- The bride's thank-you note(s) to her hostess(es) are a must.

- Thank-you notes for shower gifts received a week or two before the wedding could be delayed until after the wedding and mention of them included in the thank-you notes for wedding presents. Some feel that the bride's expressions of thanks at the shower are sufficient, and thank-you notes would go only to those who sent gifts but did not attend—others disagree.

BRIDE, BRIDESMAID, AND BACHELOR PARTIES

Entertaining the bridal couple, or the bride alone, is done in many different ways and does not require presents. Today's lifestyle makes it difficult to have the type of gala balls of yesteryear. However, reaching into the past for ways of entertaining will lessen the stress on everyone's time.

A Saturday or Sunday afternoon tea is a simple and elegant way of bringing people together. Serve tea with quartered, triangular-shaped sandwiches, scones and preserves, berries and cream, and finger pastries. Mimosas (a combination of champagne and orange juice) or cocktails are perfect optional accompaniments.

Evening cocktails served at eight during the week with nibbles and topped by fruit and ice-cream cake are suitable fare.

Another option is a buffet luncheon at noon, or, if the group is small you might have a served affair with wine to toast the bridal couple.

In Sweden, a day or two before the wedding, the bride's female friends bedeck her in a pseudo–wedding dress and a veil topped with an amusing wreath of fruit. Around her neck they place a lei of vegetables. Thus attired, they take her to a restaurant where they blithely have dinner.

A SPINSTER'S FAREWELL DINNER!

Did you know that the bride's party was once known as the spinster's farewell dinner? Apparently, it was given not to say good-bye forever to one's friends but to, er, one's spinsterhood.

It is not always feasible to follow the form laid out for who hosts what for whom; that is why the rehearsal dinner has taken on so much importance.

It is customary for the bride to entertain her bridesmaids or for them to entertain her, or both. When attendants arrive the week of the wedding, some sort of function takes place so that the group or the bride can entertain. There might not be time enough even then.

BACHELOR'S DINNER

Well, ladies, if you can have a spinster's farewell party, surely the gentlemen can have a party, er, known as a bachelor dinner. Why does the spinster's farewell have such a tragic ring to it, whereas a bachelor party is just that—a party? I'll tell you why. Picture the young maidens weeping for their maidenhood while bachelors go out on the town living it up, trying to do everything in that one evening so they can behave themselves for the rest of their lives. Gracious, could they too be weeping for their bachelorhood?

Arrangements vary, but the party is timed so that it takes place two days before the wedding. It is inadvisable and tiring to celebrate the evening before—though that is the time when most occur.

The celebration might be a dinner in a restaurant that has some form of entertainment. When the bridegroom is the guest of honor, everyone orders for himself, but the check is divided among the company, except the bridegroom.

If the festivities are at someone's home or apartment, the fare can be as simple as sandwiches and pizza along with wine and beer—or a seated meal. A popular choice is a dinner party at a club.

It is traditional for the bridegroom to propose a toast to his bride. That might be the only serious toast of the evening—the other guests offer witticisms and reminiscences.

Sometimes bachelor's and spinster's farewell parties are spontaneous. The bride and bridegroom might decide to have a joint party. If it is a gathering of attendants, gifts are presented to them and they in turn give the bridal couple the joint wedding present.

BRIDE AND BRIDESMAID PARTY

Should the bride decide to entertain her attendants, she might choose a morning coffee, a luncheon, a tea, or a dinner. It is an ideal time to present them with gifts of appreciation. If the party is held at home, then bridesmaids have a chance to see some of the wedding presents—unless the bride does not wish to display them.

PARTIES FOR GUESTS

Often, relatives and friends entertain out-of-town visitors by inviting them to lunch, afternoon tea, or dinner. It is a custom in the South and a gracious way of relieving the host family of some of the responsibility of being hospitable.

Not every family can elicit that kind of aid, so visitors must understand the family is involved in last-minute details and bear in mind that the wedding is the reason guests are in town in the first place.

It helps a great deal when the area in which the wedding celebrants live has enticing spots for sightseers and theatergoers, but it may not be possible for the family to provide escorts. Apart from attending functions specifically organized as pre-wedding entertainment, guests find their own way of amusing themselves during their free time and make their own reservations through their hotel.

Florists—
Music,
Music, Music—
Photographs

Florist

Composition is what makes a successful flower arrangement, whether you are forming a bouquet, a table display, or a vase of fresh cut flowers.

There are differences between a designer and a florist. Florists have a shop full of plants and flowers, along with sundry items such as planters and plant foods. Naturally, they also provide services for different social occasions, and some shops have designers on staff.

Flower designers do not necessarily have retail shops but go directly to markets and wholesalers for supplies. Their time goes into making arrangements for various functions, and, like designer clothes, they are more expensive.

If you want to go it alone, discuss with a local florist what blossoms and leaves show to best advantage and what flowers will be in season at the time of your wedding.

Finding a talented florist is like finding a good caterer or photographer. Get to know the person's work by looking through his or her portfolio.

When hired a year ahead, the florist can only estimate charges based on today's prices; as with the caterer, prices fluctuate depending on economic factors. If tastes lean to the unusual, you must expect prices to be higher, especially for imported or out-of-season flowers.

Your first conversation with the florist will give you an idea of the creative imagination that will go into the floral designs for your wedding.

Bud roses with sprays of baby's breath or lilies of the valley in tiny vases on cocktail tables may be just the right touch to achieve an inviting setting at an informal reception. Stately flowers at a lavish reception give the room elegance. Greenery and flowers in a house of worship bring warmth to a large area. Large formal weddings require an abundance of flowers.

The blending of colors, size, and style is important. A full, dramatic bouquet cascading down the front of a dress may hide the splendor of the wedding gown—yet, that very bouquet might set off a simple but elegant line to perfection. Tall centerpieces in the dining room might be impressive if they do not block guests from seeing one another across the table.

Suppose you have sentimental reasons for wanting to carry three long-stemmed roses. The florist's function is to understand your wishes and work the rest of the plan around the symbolic flowers.

Flowers should arrive on time and retain their fresh look for at least a week after the wedding. The bouquet is fastened so it will hold together when it flies through the air at the time when the bride tosses it to her bridesmaids. A bouquet can be made in two parts—the center bouquet is removed and the outer one is tossed.

Walk with me through a formal wedding done by a flower designer in consultation with the bride and her mother.

Marriage vows were exchanged at noon one day in May in a chapel of a well-known university. Four ficus trees in white lattice boxes flanked the altar, and the center aisle was cordoned off with wide white ribbons. White lace, entwined with miniature and bud roses centered by baby's breath, was tied together with white ribbons on the posts on both sides of the center aisle.

The sun shone through the stained-glass windows, shedding its rays on the bride's wedding dress of white tulle overlay. The gown was accented by Venice lace roses on the English net bodice and fashioned with slightly puffed sleeves, a hem edged with lace, and a cathedral train. Attached to the banded lace headdress was a fingertip veil trimmed with matching lace. Her bouquet consisted of tiny white and eggshell roses.

The bridegroom and his entourage wore gray tuxedos; his boutonniere was a white rose, and the ushers had eggshell roses.

The bridesmaids, dressed in long silver moire, carried colorful bouquets.

For the reception at a hotel, the designer had earlier arranged low centerpieces of pink and burgundy flowers with a touch of lavender here and there in two-inch-tall containers. She centered each arrangement on the mirrored dining-room tables set with burgundy cloths, pink napkins, and glass dishes. The ballroom was filled with reflected light and colors that danced back and forth from the chandeliers to the tables.

The bill, including the cost of the flowers at the rehearsal dinner, the chapel, and the reception, was expected to fall between $1,300 and $1,500.

There are so many interesting combinations that are created using candelabra, tapers, candles, flowers, and greenery. The eye is not overwhelmed by one aspect—as in a needlepoint tapestry, the colors should subtly blend.

A CALL FROM CALIFORNIA

Q: On festive or special occasions my fiancé gives me a corsage, and he insists on doing the same when we attend a friend's wedding next month. I feel uneasy about wearing one, though I am not certain why.

Only members of the bridal party carry bouquets and those honored, such as grandparents, wear corsages to distinguish them from other guests. Explain to your fiancé the impressions it'll have on the other guests and suggest he give you a lace handkerchief as an alternate keepsake.

Q: I have chosen the most beautiful centerpieces for tables at our seated dinner. How do I let people know that they are reserved and not for guests to take home? They are for special people who will not

*be able to attend the wedding: the mother of the maid of honor, who
is in the hospital; my grandmother, who is unable to come though she
lives close by; and certain other infirm relatives.*

What a lovely idea. Tag centerpieces with the names of
those who are designated to receive them.

Generally, guests don't take centerpieces without permission. It is determined by the form of entertainment. A card is
placed under a dessert plate at each table. The band leader signals the drummer to rat-a-tat-tat. The music begins while the
announcer directs the holder of the card to pass it to the third
person on the left, who then has to give it back to the second
person on the right—that person has won the centerpiece.

Music, Music, Music

"Do I know Slava? I danced at his wedding." In this old European phrase is the key to sharing the festivities of a happy
event and the memory of it. The quiet hush of the ceremony
and the burst of well-wishers afterward are a study in con-
trast—solemnity alongside joyful celebration.

The choice of wedding music depends largely on the setting
and, if held in a house of worship, on the policy of the religious
institution. Perhaps only the church organist and possibly a vocalist may perform certain approved selections, or there may
be a chanter and a choir accompaniment available. You should
discuss your preferences with the music director if you wish
pieces different from those usually offered.

The number of selections, both classical and semiclassical, is
vast. The music director may offer pieces from his or her repertoire. While it limits the selection, it also serves the purpose
of narrowing the options so it is easier to choose.

For the processional, the music is slow and dignified. Music
for the recessional is more vivacious but still dignified.

- Before the traditional Protestant wedding processional, the soft refrains of Bach, Liszt, or Beethoven fill the church as guests are being seated.
- While the wedding party walks down the aisle, the choice might be the second segment of Wagner's Bridal Chorus from *Lohengrin*, "Here Comes the Bride."
- When the organist glides into the first measure, the company rises and the bride comes into view on the arm of her father. A choir sings intermittently throughout the service and the exchange of vows might be followed by the triumphant tones of Mendelssohn's Wedding March from *A Midsummer Night's Dream*.
- Eastern Orthodox wedding hymns are sung by a choir accompanied by the organ. The choice of music is up to the priest.
- In Roman Catholic ceremonies, Gounod's or Schubert's *Ave Maria* is sung during the offertory and a quiet piece is played while the congregation prays.
- In a Jewish wedding ceremony, there may be some background music for silent prayer at midpoint. Classical composers are popular. Ultraorthodox ceremonies do not have musical accompaniment.

Musical segments from one's own culture provide a familiarity that gives comfort, strength, and a sense of unity.

MUSIC FOR THE RECEPTION

Not every couple wants the type of reception that has a lively band. Not every place for a reception—the bride's home, for example—can accommodate an area for dancing. Generally some sort of music adds to the texture of a gathering as it wafts gently through the room, filling the spaces.

You can hire a set group, a band that performs together without changes in personnel. For a party of a hundred to a hundred and fifty people, a four- or five-piece band is sufficient. Trios, duos, or soloists are best for fewer people. Instruments such as harp, viola, violin, and piano or a combination of two or more, depending on the size of the premises, work well when there is to be no dancing.

There is music for most combinations of instruments; but the largest classical repertoire is for the string quartet, which generally consists of two violins, viola, and cello; a string trio uses one violin instead of two; and a piano quartet can include piano, violin, viola, and cello.

Though there are many combinations, a woodwind trio might consist of flute, clarinet, and bassoon; flute, oboe, and bassoon; or oboe, clarinet, and French horn.

Most musical groups are combinations that play popular music and usually consist of a rhythm section, brass or woodwind, and a vocalist. The rhythm section generally comprises piano, drums, bass, and possibly a guitar, which can, if necessary, replace the piano. The brass and woodwind section can include saxophone (a saxophonist can often play clarinet or flute), trumpet, and trombone. Frequently one or several of the instrumentalists will also perform vocals and vocal harmony. Versatile groups such as these are very much in demand.

You may prefer to hire a string quartet or other classical combination for the ceremony, cocktails, and dinner, and then to bring in a dance band for lively after-dinner dancing.

Since a wedding consists of a variety of age levels, an experienced ensemble should be able to offer music of the big-band era, show and love tunes, old rock and roll, and contemporary rock and pop, as well as the appropriate ethnic tunes.

If your tastes differ, combine both preferences.

Reconsider a group that specializes in one style. If, for example, you are fans of traditional jazz and hire a Dixieland band, you run the risk of leaving out part of your company. As wonderful a musical expression as jazz is, one style of music throughout a three- or four-hour party can become monotonous.

Audition the band and band leader by attending a function or view the group's videotapes—observe how the company reacts to the band. When hosts are gracious enough to allow visitors to hear the orchestra, visitors must be as inconspicuous as possible.

Some bandleaders will take an active hand by conducting the rehearsal for the ceremony, acting as master of ceremonies for the reception, and helping coordinate events among the caterer, photographer, and band. Others take a less-visible role, preferring to limit their duties to selecting the right music as the party progresses.

A month before the wedding, give the leader a list of the music, including a selection for the first dance of the bride and bridegroom together. The leader keeps your preferences in mind. Once the party starts, the leader needs to program the music according to his best judgment, sensing the mood of the crowd and knowing how to use that rhythm to best advantage.

When playing, the maestro is aware of the situation around him and has the ability to handle the unexpected. He knows that his group is "making the event happen" when there is a full dance floor of happy, smiling faces. That vital cadence creates a happy and convivial atmosphere.

When a guest wishes to sing, an arrangement is made with the band leader about the best time to do it. Once the smoothness of the playing breaks the mood of the room in some way, it is hard to rebuild the momentum.

Groups work with slight differences. Some play for a given number of minutes per hour and then take a rest period; others play for forty-five minutes with a fifteen-minute break or work a twenty-minute set with a five-minute pause.

Continuous music means just that and the only pauses are when the maestro changes musical styles.

With the flush of a successful party, you may want the group to play not only continuously but overtime as well, which are two separate requests. Naturally, costs will increase. Playing continuously should not be a problem, but working over the contract time may not be possible because the group may have another function right after yours.

Some hosts invite the musicians to partake of the hors d'oeuvres and other food, especially if there is a buffet table. Performers wait until all the guests have served themselves.

The code of conduct that musicians observe is never eating, drinking, or smoking while onstage. Singers might discreetly have a sip of water now and then to keep in good voice.

The room arrangement should include enough space for the band to set up, and musicians should have a place to leave their cases and coats. *No one touches the musicians' instruments when they leave the bandstand on breaks*—the *least* of the damage that could be done would be upsetting the tuning system.

- As with other services, you will be asked to sign a mutually acceptable contract. Take notes.
- The information is checked carefully: wedding date, time, and places of the ceremony and reception.
- Two weeks before the wedding, the family and the bandleader discuss the details. Think carefully: *Has there been any change in wedding arrangements—such as a change of date—since the signing of the original contract?*

Even the above would not have helped recently when two weeks before the date on the contract, the bandleader read the contract out loud, confirming the wedding date, etc. The Saturday before the date on the contract, he received a frantic call from the church that the organist had not shown up. It seems that a month before, the family changed the wedding date to a week earlier but admitted that they forgot to notify him of the change. In two and a half hours the leader managed to replace one fine music group with another. The family was deeply gratified that all went smoothly.

- Contracts differ from area to area. Some reception sites require union musicians and a minimum number of hours for which they are hired.
- If you are booking through a contracting firm and like a particular leader or ensemble, you should stipulate the person(s) by name in the agreement.
- Not all groups consist of the same people at every booking, but professional local musicians with experience are able to play with most other musicians in town.
- Find the most professional group that you can afford. A friend's amateur musician son, who is paying his way through school, cannot control a complex event such as a wedding.

Not everyone realizes what a special mood live music creates at a wedding celebration, but then not everyone can afford the cost.

Another option is taped music, but you will have to spend some time gathering the appropriate selections, and you might need the advice of a musicologist.

LIVE AND RECORDED COMBOS

There is a new type of musical ensemble that combines a small live band, or even a single musician, with a prerecorded accompaniment. One of the advantages of this type of performance is that a few musicians can sound like many more. This kind of ensemble is usually not as expensive as a completely live band, but is more costly than a disc jockey.

DISC JOCKEYS

Disc jockeys bring stereo equipment with amplifiers and speakers designed to fill a large room without distortion. The DJ's selections are organized so he or she can quickly select any tune.

Some disc jockeys supply mood lighting and may or may not act as a master of ceremonies.

Photographs

Unlike the wedding dress, which is stored away in a box to gather dust in the attic, the wedding album is enjoyed for more than a lifetime. Photographs of the most significant day of your life take on an even greater meaning as time passes—both in terms of the sweetness of life and the sadness of it. At the very least, those faces that look back at us are living remembrances in which future generations can take pleasure.

One of the pitfalls is hiring an amateur photographer who has not the foggiest idea of what constitutes an album that tells the story of the wedding day. Even if the photographer is excellent, the most important question is whether he or she has experience in shooting the events of the wedding day.

As with any specialty, recommendations from friends are helpful. If the photographer is with a studio, the contract is issued in the firm's name, but his name is written into the contract as the person photographing the wedding. However, that person may be unavailable on your wedding day.

Most photographers do their best to provide a fair contract with everything detailed, and then present fine albums for families to treasure.

GUIDELINES
- A photographer should be able to unobtrusively perform his work.
- Ask the clergyman about rules governing the taking of photographs during the ceremony. Some houses of worship do not allow the filming of certain parts of the wedding ceremony.

- Question the photographer about his or her portfolio. Note the sequence of events when studying the albums.
- Ask the photographer how he or she likes to work:

  For your *formal wedding portrait,* some feel there is no look that can match the radiance of a bride on her wedding day. The photographer either comes to the house when the bride is dressed or does the job before the reception.

  Others prefer to take the formal portrait of the bride on the day she goes for the fitting of her bridal gown.

  Still another suggests that both bring their bridal clothes to the studio after the wedding, where the lighting and the background are controlled.

- Have formal shots of the wedding party taken before you are tired and look wilted.
- If the family does not want photographs taken of guests, other than those specified, *list that in the contract.* The couple might rightly be nervous at the possibility that an important part of the festivities could be missed because the photographer was busy elsewhere—it has happened. Change of instructions would come only from the bride and her parents. Any requests should be referred to them.
- Prepare a list of the type of pictures wanted during each phase of the wedding, including both formal and informal shots. The photographer needs to know what you expect.
- Have a balanced picture story of the event from beginning to end, including both the bride and bridegroom, both families and friends.
- To engage the services of a studio, a contract is drawn and signed by both parties. Be sure to take it home and look it over carefully. Ask if there are any charges, and check to see that the quoted price is what you had agreed upon.

  Check the time and date of the wedding. Pencil in the changes needed, initial each one, and return the contract to the photographer, but keep the copy.

  There may be a clause that says that the photographer

is allowed to eat or rest after a certain number of hours of work—that is a reasonable request. He comes early to the wedding site; the job starts immediately, and he works almost nonstop until the wedding is over.

- Sometime after the wedding the photographer will telephone to say the proofs are ready. He might show all the successful shots on a contact sheet, from which the couple makes their selection for the final album. I prefer the proof method, because each photograph is about three inches by four inches and clear to the naked eye. Although contact sheets are less expensive, the photographs on the contact sheet are small and it is hard to see details.

- Of the three albums, one is a complete record for the bridal couple. Their parents might like a complete album or choose one consisting of the events before and during the ceremony, but have the rest of the photographs of their respective families and friends. Also, list the names of the guests on the back of each photograph so that, as the years go by, future generations will know their identities.

- A photograph album can be placed on a compact disk in a format called Kodak Photo-CD, which is viewed on either a computer that is properly equipped or a new device called the CD Interactive. By the time this book is published, there will probably be other formats, such as the newly developed technology called multimedia.

VIDEOTAPING

Videotaping is a rapidly changing technology. A handheld video camera, with incredible sensitivity to light, now makes it possible to achieve videotapes of good quality without the need of bright lights.

Manufacturers keep developing more sophisticated equipment, both in terms of cameras and sound, so I can write only about what is going on at the moment.

Current videotape formats are, among others, 8mm, VHS, and S-VHS. (Many people still have Beta machines, but the format is no longer manufactured.) The sizes of the tapes are different, so the firm that does the work must be able to make copies in either format. Copies can be made from the original without losing too much color and depth. It is also possible to make a copy from another copy.

Videotaping is understandably popular. The results are seen almost immediately. Although it is somewhat similar to photography, it is informal and spontaneous. But in no way does videotaping take the place of those beautiful stills that capture a particular moment. In any case, both have their unique value.

With permission of the officiant, the videographer can tape the entire wedding ceremony.

At the reception he tapes the events, concentrating on the instructions from the family. He interviews guests at the reception who say a few words, possibly editing those who have imbibed too many drinks. When viewed later, the event is seen as it happened, rather than as highlights.

Videotaping services may be provided by the photography studio; they are likely to engage a talent equal to the standards of their firm. Either way, the contract rules are the same as for the musicians and photographers—the videographer should have the same privileges.

As with a photographer, a videographer is required to unobtrusively tape various scenes that make the festivities into a living memory. The shooting should be done so subtly that people are unaware they are being filmed, except during interviews with guests.

Alert the videographer of a change of plan during the party. As with the photographer, a missed scene can never be repeated.

The end product should be tastefully edited—not even Uncle Thomas wants to see Uncle Thomas standing on his ear. Guests must be discreet when being interviewed. A videographer told me that the mother of the bride made a derogatory remark about her ex-husband. When she realized the remark was there for posterity, she asked that it be deleted from the tape.

If a tape is too dark, it can be made lighter. There are companies that can restore or doctor a tape so that it looks highly professional.

The Wedding Ceremony

*T*here is something comforting about the familiar, and so we stick to customs and traditions often without knowing how or why they began. This is particularly true of weddings as well as receptions. Tradition sets weddings apart from any other function. The engaged couple, while looking forward to the future, become enwrapped by the wedding customs of the past. For many their marriage becomes the first step in their recognition of their place in the scheme of things.

My walk through the different religious and nonreligious wedding ceremonies has been a special experience—the poetic words that reach the very depth of our cultures . . .

. . . Dearly beloved, we are assembled here in the presence of God . . . Man should leave his father and mother and cleave unto his wife . . . One of the joyous occasions declared "very good" by the Creator . . . Thou art consecrated unto me . . . I take thee to be my lawfully wedded wife/husband . . . To cherish a mutual esteem and love . . . In honesty and industry to provide for each . . . To live together as the heirs of the grace of life . . . Speaking out of the silence . . . For time and for eternity . . . Who gives their blessing? We, her parents . . . Since it is your intention . . . May the Lord bless you and keep you . . .

And so I invite readers to look into the window not only of their own backgrounds, but also of others. The need is great in this changing world with the increase in ecumenical and interfaith marriages.

You are fortunate that some customs have disappeared. Imagine being in ancient Rome standing next to your beloved, in wedding clothes, silently pledging vows in front of witnesses. The augur divines signs for the success of the marriage by sacrificing an animal to the gods. After examining the poor creature's entrails, he pronounces the gods' approval, or, in some cases, disapproval.

Now imagine yourself in the fourteenth century where English marriage rites are fortuitous. If the betrothal contract follows consummation, it is binding by the church and the community. A child born before the actual marriage but after the betrothal is legitimate. With no formal guidelines, bigamy is rampant because of the absence of any kind of registry or formal ceremony.

Your marriage may not be entered into by your own free will but through pressure from other sources, arranged between families for political and financial gain. Your parents might not feel you have to bend to their will, but they view romantic love with one's spouse as a development that comes after marriage (not so different from some cultures today). Marrying into a family at the same social level is of prime importance. A mismatched couple may displease the Crown and completely ruin a family's connections, and spell financial disaster.

Despite the possibility of putting your affluent family in jeopardy, you elope to escape your parents' choice of a marriage partner. You end up with a fortune hunter or worse and married by a clergyman of dubious reputation. The church tries to control those clergymen but with little success. You would not want to do that to your parents, would you?

Now you are in the middle of the fifteenth century. Though teachings on marriage are in the New Testament, and Old Testament centuries before, it is now that the church views marriage as a sacrament. You have to wait another century for vows spoken in front of a Catholic priest and laws passed requiring the registration of births, marriages, and deaths.

The seventeenth century tightens laws governing marriage, though it was not until your journey into the eighteenth century that the British Parliament passed the Marriage Act affecting the entire country. For those with means, a written financial contract is drawn up between the marrying families, generally to give the bride some protection if her husband dies or deserts her. Witnesses are present and oral promises exchanged, banns are posted three consecutive times, a religious ceremony takes place, and, finally, consummation . . . and before you know it, you're married!

But this is the here and now. . . .

A civil marriage ceremony can be arranged in a week, or a formal wedding can take as much as a year to arrange.

The time of day or evening when the wedding occurs depends on the location. Evening weddings are more popular in the South and Southwestern states, a custom necessitated by the sultry climate and before the advent of air-conditioning. Northern and Eastern states tend to favor afternoon weddings between four and five o'clock.

Jewish weddings can be held any day of the week, except during the Sabbath between sundown on Friday and sundown on Saturday, and generally take place on Saturday evening—which means they start quite late during the summer—Sunday noon, and Sunday evening.

It seems that hats for women are optional in most Christian churches, though at one time they were required.

Below is the basic form of protocol and custom for weddings . . .

Programs

Programs for weddings serve as a schedule of the marriage ceremony process and are handed by ushers to guests as they enter the house of worship. The printer has examples that will be helpful. Programs may be printed on inexpensive paper, but many are handsomely designed to match the color and quality of the wedding invitation. The cover may be elegantly embossed with the words "Our Wedding Program" and the names of the bride- and bridegroom-elect.

The next page is headed by the names of the bridal couple, the date and time of the wedding, and the names of the church and the city. Line for line, the name and the function of each participant appears.

Pew Cards

Occasionally a large, stop-the-traffic wedding takes place requiring the use of pew cards. They go to the closest members of the bridal couple's family and friends. The cards are inserted with the wedding invitations or, if the family needs to know precisely how many pews to cordon off, they are sent after acceptances are received.

The cards are printed or handwritten on at-home cards or small firm blank cards—pew number, optional:

> *Within the ribbons*
> *printed names of the host and hostess*

When guests enter the church, those with cards show them to escorting ushers.

Protestant Ceremony

The Protestant marriage ceremony may vary from one denomination to the other. It is taken from the *Book of Common Prayer* and is the basis and the very depth of the Protestant Christian philosophy on marriage. The ceremony begins with:

The Persons to be married shall present themselves before the Minister, the Man standing on the right hand of the Woman. Then, all present reverently standing, the Minister shall say:

. . . if either of you know any reason ye may not be lawfully joined together in marriage, in the covenant of their God . . .

With those words the couple face the minister, who reads the opening in the familiar language:

Dearly beloved, we are assembled here in the presence of God to join this Man and this Woman in holy marriage; which is instituted of God, regulated by His commandments, blessed by our Lord Jesus Christ, and to be held in honor among all men. Let us, therefore, reverently remember that God has established and sanctified marriage, for the welfare and happiness of mankind . . .

Though the substance of the marriage ceremony remains the same, there are minor changes in method incorporated within the ceremony that indicate the preferences of the particular denomination, church, and minister.

And now on to the pattern of the wedding day . . .

If you live in a busy city, allow enough driving time to the house of worship in case there is heavy traffic.

Guests arrive at the church or ceremony site not later than thirty minutes before the ceremony starts.

The bridegroom, best man, and the attendants arrive thirty minutes early.

The maid or matron of honor leaves the bride's home after she and the bride's mother have helped the bride dress.

The bridegroom's parents come about fifteen minutes before the ceremony begins.

The bride and her father also arrive no less than fifteen before the ceremony and wait in the minister's office.

Traditionally, the bride's family and guests sit on the left of the aisle and the bridegroom's people on the right.

Ushers stand at the entrance of the church to escort ladies to their seats after asking which side of the family they know. The lady takes the usher's extended right arm, while the gentleman walks slightly behind—their children follow. When guests arrive all at once and time is short, the usher extends his arm to the senior lady, asking the others to follow.

While the soloist is singing, guests stand at the entrance until the rendition is over.

Some houses of worship have a center aisle and two side aisles. The center aisle is for immediate family—brothers, sisters, grandparents, aunts, and uncles.

Depending on the size of the list, guests sit in the center or side pews.

The ceremony is about to begin when the bridegroom's mother, on the arm of the head usher, is led to the first pew on the right of the aisle. The bridegroom's father follows.

When the bride's mother, escorted by the head usher, is seated in the first pew on the left side of the aisle, the door to the church closes and the ceremony begins. Latecomers wait until the bride's mother is seated, then go discreetly to the side aisles in the back.

Guests seated early have the choice of seats, and those who arrive afterward should not expect them to move.

If the bride's parents are divorced and her mother has remarried, her stepfather sits with her mother in the first pew. Her father goes to the third pew where his wife, if he has remarried, is seated. The same applies to the bridegroom's divorced parents.

The head usher alerts the bridesmaids and groomsmen to take their places for the processional.

If there is to be a canvas runner, two ushers roll it out immediately after the bride's mother takes her seat. Ushers start at the foot of the chancel and unroll the runner up the aisle. Sometimes, the runner is laid before the ceremony and guests are escorted from either side of the aisle.

The processional starts with the music chosen for the occasion.

Entering the sanctuary, the minister goes up the steps to the chancel and faces the congregation.

In most denominations the company sits during the ceremony and stands when the officiant reads prayers and hymns.

The bridegroom enters from the sacristy, followed two paces behind by his best man, and stands at the right foot of the chancel with the best man slightly behind and to the right of him as they face the officiant. They then turn at right angles to the company as the processional starts so that the bridegroom may watch his bride come toward him.

The organist gives a musical clue to the first attendants so they arrive at their appointed place on time. At a steady gait, they start with the left foot, each pair about four paces ahead of the next—depending on the length of the church and the number of attendants. As they arrive at the altar they separate, left and right; or they may all stand on one side.

There are many possible variations in these arrangements; the officiant and assistant know best how the procession should proceed in their church.

The maid of honor is next. She stands opposite the best man on the left of the chancel. If there is a matron of honor, she places herself slightly back from the maid.

Preceding the bride and her father, the flower girl walks down the aisle while scattering petals from a basket—with the permission of the officiant. The ring bearer, holding the cushion with the ring secured to it, may walk with the flower girl. When they reach the chancel they separate. If they are old enough, the flower girl stands alongside or slightly behind the maid of honor; the ring bearer stands by the best man, who has relieved the ring bearer of his burden. Or, they sit with their respective parents. Meanwhile, the company turns in the direction of the bride as she and her father begin their walk to the sanctuary.

The bride takes her father's right arm and holds her bouquet below her waist in her other hand. The company stands as the chords of the nuptial march fill the sanctuary. The bride and her father stand still for a moment before proceeding, left foot first, down the aisle to the foot of the chancel. At this point, the bride might give her father a kiss as he releases her arm.

Meanwhile, the bridegroom steps forward, reaching out to his bride, who places her bouquet in her left hand. Together they face the minister, who places the bride's hand in the bridegroom's.

As the actual service begins, the bride gives her bouquet to the maid of honor so her left hand is free to receive the ring. If the maid of honor is holding the bridegroom's ring, she should have a convenient stand on which to place the bouquet; but if there is a matron of honor, she holds the bridal bouquet.

If the "giving away" of the bride is included, her father remains where he is. The minister asks: "Who giveth this woman to be married to this man?" Her father steps forward and places his daughter's hand in the minister's, and says, "I do," or "Her mother and I do." If her mother participates, she stands and jointly both say: "We do." He then goes to the first pew and sits next to his wife. (Some services omit this part.)

The best man hands the ring to the minister for the blessing. The bridegroom takes the ring from the minister and puts it on the bride's finger.

The minister declares, "I now pronounce you husband and wife." If the bride wears a veil, the bridegroom lifts it for the bridal kiss.

The bride, still facing the minister, takes her bouquet from the maid of honor. As the newlyweds turn and face the company, the bride's attendant straightens the train. Then the couple goes up the aisle to the joyful music of the recessional march. The flower girl follows. The best man and maid of honor along with the attendants—couple by couple—follow the bride and bridegroom up the aisle.

At this point in a military wedding there is the Arch of Swords ceremony.

The ushers return swiftly to complete their duties. First the head usher escorts the bride's mother, followed by her husband. The bridegroom's mother takes the arm of the head usher, if there is one, and walks up the aisle followed by her husband. Single grandmothers should also be escorted by an usher.

I prefer that the parents of the bride walk together, followed by the bridegroom's parents. To me it equates the steps of nurturing parents to the first steps their children take as husband and wife.

Ushers discreetly wait with guests until the entire wedding party has reached the vestibule. Only then do guests leave in turn—row by row, the front pews first.

Whether or not the photographer was allowed to shoot during the ceremony, he certainly may do so during the Arch of Swords/Sabers ceremony and the recessional. The couple wait in the vestry with their parents and the bridal party until the entire church empties. Then the photo session begins. The photographer has the bridal couple and the bridal party retrace the ceremony, with the clergyperson participating. Shots should include the couple leaving the church.

The best man then accompanies the bride and bridegroom to the limousine or to their car, which he drives.

In the meantime, the bridesmaids and the parents of the bride and bridegroom all meet at the reception site.

Lutheran

In the Lutheran tradition, those attending a marriage ceremony are not only invited guests but are participants in a service of worship—one of the joyous occasions declared "very good" by the Creator.

Marriage is a social contract of commitment. It is the couple who perform the marriage, since they marry each other; the minister represents both the church and the state, attesting that they have made their religious and legal statements in both areas. The basic elements of Lutheran philosophy regarding marriage are fidelity and "steadfast love" on which marriage is founded, not passion.

Most elements of the marriage ceremony are flexible and are discussed by the pastor prior to the wedding. Most ministers are willing to work with the couple to provide either a more traditional or contemporary service. The tradition of the "giving away" ceremony is up to the bridal couple. Parents may accompany their children in the procession, read the lessons, stand behind them as vows are exchanged, and take part in the blessing.

Some congregations use the "exchanging of the peace," in which the minister says: "The peace of the Lord be with you."

The congregation responds: "And also with you."

The minister intones: "Let us now share that peace with each other."

It is rare to celebrate Holy Communion in wedding services, but if the couple wish to include it, the ceremony precedes Communion.

Quaker

There are four branches of Friends or Quakers in the United States. Each group conducts meetings somewhat differently. Contrary to general belief, some branches do have ministers and use the standard Protestant form of marriage rites.

The Friends General Conference and Conservative branch conduct weddings in the classical tradition of Quakers, since each member is a minister and their signatures are recognized in the United States as legally binding on a marriage certificate.

To be married within the Friends Meeting, petitioners must

be known to the Community of Friends and their union is investigated by the Clearness Committee.

Approval comes from the whole meeting, for the couple come under the care of Friends, as the name suggests, who assume an obligation for them throughout their lives—as that couple will for other Friends.

A Friend may marry a non-Friend. The meeting takes place at home or in the regular Friends meeting place. The simplicity of the meeting site matches the simplicity of the way members come together in silent contemplation, until someone "speaks out of the silence."

The wedding is incorporated into the events of the meeting especially called for that purpose. All is quiet for a while until the bridal couple stand to exchange marriage vows and wedding rings.

The original phrasing of the pledge is still the one most chosen by marrying couples:

In the presence of God and these our friends, I take thee, ———, to be my wedded wife [husband], promising with Divine assistance to be unto thee a loving and faithful husband [wife] as long as we both shall live.

After making the pledge and exchanging rings, they sit down. Relatives bring a table bearing the marriage certificate and place it in front of the newlyweds. They sign their names and the document is read aloud. The meeting ends when one person turns to another to shake hands. All are welcome to sign the marriage certificate. A reception follows, which might be held on the lawn of the meeting house or at a home. Generally, the congregation joins in the preparations.

Mormon

The betrothed must be members in good standing to be married in a temple of the Church of Jesus Christ of Latter-Day Saints. That means they have met the religious qualifications, paid tithes, and served within the church for two years.

Because temple ordinances are not discussed and the teachings are implicative, the written material available to outsiders does not specify what constitutes the actual wedding ceremony or the wording of the exchange of vows.

For the ceremony, the couple don white temple clothing. The service takes the form of a sealing ordinance in the "sealing" room that joins the bridal couple symbolically for "time and for eternity"—time on earth and after death. The ceremony is performed by a bishop, a stake president, or a sealer.

The bridal couple can invite relatives and friends closest to them. However, the "good standing" rule applies to guests as well. One or both sets of parents may not be qualified to witness the temple marriage of their child, but they are invited to the festivities afterwards in the visitors' center.

Mormons who are not in good standing may be married in a "civil" ceremony—that is also a religious event, despite its name—by bishops of the church that takes place in a room at the visitor's center.

Seventh-Day Adventist

Rarely do Seventh-Day Adventists marry on Saturday, since that is their Sabbath. The wedding ceremony itself is a religious event, so it may take place on Saturday as part of the basic worship service. When the reception follows the ceremony, the event becomes a secular one and unacceptable; therefore, most weddings take place on Sunday instead.

Rites are based on the Protestant wording, but there is no prescribed ceremony as such. The church encourages simple weddings in keeping with the meaning of marriage. The pastor reads one of the several sermonettes the couple has chosen from *The Manual for Ministers.*

Then the pastor asks:
   Who gives their blessing to this marriage?
Sometimes her parents respond:
   We, her parents.
On other occasions, every member of the family, on both sides, stands and says:
   We, the families.

The ring has not been part of the marriage ceremony of the North American Adventist Church. Wearing jewelry, though not forbidden, is rare among Adventists.

There are some pastors who will not take part in an ecumenical ceremony. Others might participate in a limited way, possibly administering a blessing and directing a personal talk to the bridal couple. The minister for the other religion would perform the actual ceremony.

Roman Catholic

Roman Catholic weddings take place at various times during the day. The very formal wedding is celebrated before noon or at noon during High Mass, when there is a choir to offer liturgical music. Others might have the ceremony at Low Mass as early as eight or nine o'clock in the morning. Catholics may marry on Sunday before six in the evening. Marriages during Lent or Advent are cleared with the priest.

The Mass is the center of the Catholic Church, and the Sacrament of Marriage may take place within the Mass; the combination of both together is the Nuptial Mass. The ceremony, performed between two Catholics, takes about fifty minutes. It may take place anytime during the day whether or not there is a Mass, except during the times for confession. Weddings sometimes take place on Saturday evening.

A traditional marriage ceremony requires the bride's home church, a priest, and the sacrament. Special permission is necessary if the couple wish to marry in another parish.

As with almost every wedding, it is advisable to start planning early, especially during popular months.

The priest's guidance on the ceremony itself is important, since each church has its own guidelines within the bounds of the Rite of Marriage. He also advises where attendants will stand during the marriage rites, on the suitability of musical selections, the taking of photographs, and floral arrangements.

First the priest offers prayers in which the names of the bridal couple are mentioned, followed by readings from Scripture. If the ceremony is a Mass, one of the readings must be from the Gospel, while the others can be from the Old or the New Testaments. The first two readings are by close family members. After a five-minute sermon, there is the exchange of vows.

A marriage between a Catholic and a non-Catholic can take place in the church. However, the Mass is omitted from the traditional marriage rites as well as kneeling for the Blessing of the Rings and the Exchange of Rings.

With the permission of the Catholic Church, a Catholic may marry a non-Catholic in the church of another denomination. The applicant petitions the archdiocese in which the Catholic lives for Matrimonial Dispensation. If granted, the Catholic priest will be able to participate in an ecumenical ceremony.

There are stipulations: With the knowledge of the non-Catholic partner, the Catholic partner must promise, either orally or in writing, to bring up the children as Catholics. The marrying Catholic has then met form and consent: "form" means that the priest has been involved and may also have witnessed or concelebrated the marriage; "consent" means that the marriage was not entered out of fear, coercion, or immaturity.

And so, after the Nuptial Mass the newly married couple leaves the church with the phrases exchanged between them and the priest . . .

Since it is your intention to enter into marriage . . .
I promise to be true in good times and bad, in sickness and health . . .
What God has joined, men must not divide . . .

Jewish

There are three disciplines in the practice of Judaism in America: Orthodox—the most traditional; Reform—most influenced by Western society; and Conservative—a bridge between the other two. Marriage customs have their core in four thousand years of Jewish history combined with customs of the country in which the family lives.

In recent years there have been subtle changes in the cultural differences within the Conservative and Reform disciplines. I am told that some Conservative synagogues have become more liberal and the Reform Temples are more accepting of some of the traditional customs. It is especially true for the wedding ceremony. However, much depends on the rabbi and the bridal couple.

In the Orthodox synagogues, men and women sit in separate sections. Men and women sit together in some Conservative synagogues, but both Orthodox and Conservatives require that women wear hats or small circular lace head coverings and men wear skullcaps (yarmulkes).

In Reform temples, men and women sit together; neither need wear hats.

All guests should follow whichever dress code applies.

The bride's family sits on the right of the aisle and the bridegroom's family on the left. With the exception of the first and second rows, guests from both families are free to sit where they please.

One of the prewedding honors, the "Aufruf," takes place on the Saturday, Monday, or Thursday before the wedding, at which the bridegroom reads the Torah and in some congregations the future bride may also take part.

The superstition against the bride being seen in her wedding gown by the bridegroom before the wedding is not part of Jewish folklore. In Orthodox and some Conservative and Reform disciplines, the bridal couple and their families meet in an anteroom for the Veiling of the Bride (*badeken*). The bride is veiled, like the biblical Rebekah. The bridegroom lowers the veil once he sees that the bride is truly his beloved—unlike the biblical Jacob who thought he had married Rachel only to find it was her older sister, Leah, under the veil.

There is no set rule for the processional, and so there are many variations—depending perhaps on what the rabbi advises, the size of the wedding party, the possible complication of divorced parents, and the preferences of the couple.

The rabbi and the cantor walk down the aisle and stand under the four-cornered marriage canopy (*huppah*), decorated with flowers and greenery. It is positioned before the raised platform leading to the Ark (*bimah*). If the wedding takes place elsewhere, they walk to an estrade where the ceremony takes place under the canopy.

In front of the rabbi is a cloth-covered wedding table on which are the ritual wineglasses, the wrapped glass for breaking, and the ketubah (the marriage contract).

Both families honor grandparents and great-grandparents by including them in the preprocessional walk down the aisle— they sit with their respective families. If there are great aunts and uncles, they walk down the aisle before the grandparents. A member of the family escorts a single grandmother, but a single grandfather should have a choice of whether or not he walks alone; he might appreciate his child or grandchild doing the honors.

The procession of the bridesmaids and ushers is similar to most American weddings. There are some differences from that point on.

The best man follows and waits at the left of the marriage canopy for the bridegroom, who walks with his mother on his right and his father on his left. He stands on the rabbi's left awaiting the bride. His parents stand near or under the canopy.

The maid or matron of honor walks down the aisle and stands on the right side under the canopy to await the arrival of the bride.

The bride, her face veiled, takes her father's right arm; her mother walks next to her on the opposite side. At the canopy she takes her place on her bridegroom's right while her parents stand to the right.

In some Orthodox ceremonies the fathers escort the bridegroom and stand near him; the mothers accompany the bride and stand with her. In the Sephardic tradition, the mothers walk seven times around the bride, and in some traditions the bride walks around the bridegroom.

The Reform and some Conservatives follow the American custom for the procession.

There are specific dates during the Jewish calendar year when a rabbi is not permitted to perform marriages. The longest period lasts forty-nine days, except for one or two days within that span, and is from Passover to the Feast of Weeks (Shavuot). Check with the rabbi about the dates on which marriages are prohibited.

The Hebrew calendar, unlike the Gregorian, is based on the lunar month of twenty-eight and a half days.

Most Jewish weddings take place Saturday evening or Sunday afternoon or evening. Because the Sabbath begins at sundown on Friday evening and ends at sundown on Saturday, a Saturday evening wedding in the summertime starts quite late.

A wedding can take place on any day of the week except Saturday or during a religious observance. Neither Orthodox, Conservative, nor Reform rabbis will marry a Jew to a non-Jew. At this writing, it is possible to find a rabbi who will participate in an interfaith ceremony, but most rabbis refuse.

Although divorce is accepted by all disciplines, all Orthodox and most Conservative rabbis will not marry anyone who has not obtained a Jewish divorce, called a "get."

Reform rabbis, recognizing civil divorce, do not insist on a Jewish divorce.

Rabbis will gladly perform a religious ceremony for a couple who were married in a civil ceremony. Since the legal part is fulfilled, only the religious phase is performed, including the signing of the marriage contract, the giving of the ring, and the seven blessings. At least ten men (a minyan) must be present at the ceremony.

There are two parts to the ceremony: the betrothal and the marriage ceremony. The betrothal includes the signing of the Jewish marriage contract, which takes place before the ceremony in a private room. It is attended by the rabbi, the bridegroom, the bride, both sets of parents, and two men not related to the family. The men also serve as witnesses to the public marriage ceremony in which the bride is given the wedding ring.

The reading aloud of the marriage contract, which is written in Aramaic—the ancient language of commerce—is always included in Orthodox and in some Conservative and Reform ceremonies.

Today, though the wedding ceremony is a religious one and hailed with joy, in the Jewish tradition, marriage is considered a civil arrangement between two families.

The ceremony is traditionally conducted in Hebrew, the language of the Bible. Many rabbis chant the prayers in Hebrew and read them in English.

The first cup of wine from which the bride and bridegroom

drink is followed by the giving of the ring. The bridegroom puts it on the forefinger of the bride's right hand. Later the bride may want to place it on the third finger of her left hand. In some Conservative and all Reform ceremonies, the bride and bridegroom exchange wedding rings.

The rabbi speaks some personal words to the bridal couple just before or just after the Seven Blessings, which come from the Talmud—an ancient collection of Jewish moral laws and tradition.

The ceremony concludes when the rabbi hands the glass to the best man, who places it on the floor so that the bridegroom can crush it with his right foot—hoping it will shatter the first time. Some sources say it is a remembrance of the destruction of the temple of Solomon in Jerusalem by the Babylonians. Others interpret it as a symbolic act of purification—the bride and bridegroom come to each other free of the past.

The ceremony now is over, and the congregation responds with "Mazel Tov," which means "Good luck" or "Congratulations."

And so the ancient words have again been repeated: *"Thou art consecrated unto me with this ring . . ."* And again, *"The voice of joy and gladness . . ."*

East Indian Traditional Hindu Wedding

Single Hindu men and women might be introduced by relatives or friends, or they might meet at a gathering. They have two to three dates. If by the third date, they feel drawn to each other, their families—after obtaining information about each other's backgrounds and the suitability of the match—arrange a meeting. There is a short engagement period, and the wedding takes place within a few months.

Two days before the wedding, the Hindu bride (*dulhan*) and

the bridegroom (*dhula*) go through a welcoming ceremony at the bride's family home attended by her relatives, friends, the bridegroom, and his close family members.

Part of the celebration for the event is the Mehendi henna. A relative or friend paints a design on the bride's palms, fingernails, and feet with a henna preparation—a tradition followed by many religions in the East. During the Mehendi henna, guests dance and sing the familiar songs of India. When the henna painting is complete the bride joins in the festivities, which include refreshments.

The henna is made of finely crushed leaves from the turmeric plant found in East India. To add the rich red color, dried tea leaves—after boiling and straining—are mixed with the turmeric. The last ingredient is lemon juice or tamarind water, which is thoroughly stirred into the mixture until it becomes a paste. (Turmeric is also used as a condiment and has medicinal values.)

The day before the wedding the couple do not see each other so that they will be rested for the wedding day.

On their special day, the bridegroom and some members of his family arrive at the bride's parents' home. The bridegroom's clothing consists of a *turban*, attached in the front by a gold or silver sheer veil called a *sehra*, which covers his face; a *sherwani*—a long, buttoned, high-collared coat; and a *churidar pajama*—a gathered silk brocaded tight-fitting pair of pants.

The bride might wear the traditional *sari*, made of heavily embroidered brocaded silk, with its six yards draped over her head or over one shoulder. Or she might wear a *ghagra*—a loose vertical pleated skirt worn just below the navel and flowing down to the ankles; a *choli*—a half-sleeved bodice or jacket; and an *orhni*—a transparent head shawl that falls gracefully down her back. However, she may wish to wear Western clothes.

For the Jaymala welcoming wedding ceremony, relatives and friends gather once again at the entrance of the bride's parents' home, where the bride and bridegroom exchange flowered garlands.

The site for the Havan Kund wedding ceremony is decorated whether it is in the house itself or the garden. The couple sit on pillows. The Hindu priest (Pandit ji) sits in front of the Havan, a vessel housing a burning fire, and reads a portion of the Holy Book. He then recites one of four vows, including loyalty in sickness and in health and shared responsibilities. The bridal couple toss fruits, seeds, water, and flowers—the symbols of daily life—into the fire. The bride and bridegroom walk four times around the fire. Each time the Pandit ji recites from the Holy Book. The ceremony is then completed.

Blessings are bestowed on the bridal couple by his parents, her parents, and by each relative. This part of the ceremony is comparable to the Western receiving line.

The bridegroom brings his bride to his parents' house. To show the family respect, the bride is received by his parents along with aunts and uncles who shower her with praise, flowers, and congratulations.

Greek (Eastern) Orthodox

The Orthodox Church does not allow any changes in the ancient Sacrament of Marriage. A license to marry is obtained from the church itself as well as the usual license from the state.

A chanter responds to the petitions of the priest during the ceremony. The organ is used during the processional and recessional.

The ceremony may be conducted either in English or in the native tongue of the church of origin—Greek, Russian, Romanian, or Bulgarian.

In the United States, the bride and the bridegroom stand in front of and very close to the altar table.

The bridegroom is led by the best man to the altar. The bride is escorted by her father, and so the first part of the ceremony begins.

In the Betrothal Service, the bride and bridegroom hold lighted candles as the priest invokes the blessings. It continues with references to the Old and New Testaments.

The rings are exchanged with the aid of the sponsor (*koumbaros*), who must be a member of the church in good standing. The sponsor will offer moral support to the bridal couple throughout their married lives and is the official witness to the marriage. According to folklore, the bridegroom's ring symbolizes the sun and the bride's ring, the moon.

The priest, with both rings in his hand, presses the foreheads of the bride and bridegroom three times, each time intoning the name of the Holy Trinity. Because the right hand has a rich symbolic meaning in the Church, he places the rings on the third fingers of their right hands.

Part of the Sacrament of Marriage is the Exchange of Crowns, in which the priest crowns the bride and the bridegroom. The crowns are made of white beads and joined in the back by white ribbons. With their hands clasped together, he leads them three times around the altar in a ritual dance, which predates Christianity and is part of both Cultic and Judaic practice. The dance around the altar table, which contains the Gospel Book, is a reminder of the dance around the Ark of the Covenant.

Weddings may take place any day of the week. The periods in which weddings are not performed are from December 13 through Christmas Day; Epiphany Day and the day before it; August 1 through 15 (Fast of the Holy Theotokos); during Great Lent, Holy Week, and Easter Sunday; and on Pentecost and major feast days.

If the Orthodox Christian marries outside the Church's jurisdiction, the Orthodox Christian puts him or herself out of communication with the Church. A state of grace is restored if the rites take place later.

The marriage of an Eastern Orthodox Christian to a baptized non-Orthodox Christian is considered "mixed" but the wedding ceremony may take place in the Church. A marriage between a Greek Orthodox Christian and a nonbaptized person is not allowed.

The Orthodox Church is headed by its own Archbishop and is separate from the Roman Catholic Church. A divorce is granted by the Orthodox Church by special petition, but only after a civil divorce has been obtained.

And so the voices echo the ancient phrase, *Na zisete!* May you live!

African American

"Jumping the broom" is a recent addition to some African American wedding ceremonies, regardless of the denomination in which the couple exchange marriage vows. Some couples decorate a broom with ribbons and bows and the officiant incorporates the meaning of it into his or her sermon.

While the importance of the broomstick may have its roots in Africa, the jumping of the broom has become symbolic, to some, of those years when a religious legal marriage was not permitted—a reminder of how ancestors were brought to the United States as slaves and how they fared.

The wedding ceremony consisted of placing a broom on the ground. The bride and bridegroom jumped over the broom and thereby became husband and wife.

Weddings in the United States Armed Forces

Those in the armed forces, like civilians, have to arrange for a house of worship whether on base or in the civilian community. They decide whether to have a formal or informal wedding, what type of reception to arrange, and whom and how many people to invite.

Not every bridal couple has a military chapel wedding but either way, as in civilian life, the couple has to arrive at a date that suits both them and their families. The arrangements depend on where each is stationed.

The couple must notify the branch of service in which they serve of their impending change of status.

A servicewoman has the choice of keeping her own name or of assuming her husband's. However, she must complete a form from the personnel department regarding her name change.

If stationed in a foreign country, ask the chaplain how to obtain information about the marriage laws of the country.

There are rules and procedures to follow if a serviceman or woman wants to marry a foreign national. Will your fiancé(e)'s government give permission to marry and to leave his or her native country? What are the immigration laws for entering the United States? The information may be obtained through the chaplain's office. You may be directed to the adjutant's office for questions on immigration.

DRESS CODE

When a member of the armed forces wears his or her uniform, only military medals and insignias are displayed on the jacket.

The bride has the option of wearing a wedding dress or being married in uniform—in either case she carries a bouquet.

The bridegroom has the option of wearing his uniform or the appropriate civilian wear (tuxedo or business suit). If he wears civilian clothes, a boutonniere is appropriate. He and the best man wear the type of attire suitable to the formality of the wedding, the time of year, and whether it is a day or evening wedding.

AIR FORCE
- Mess dress is the *most formal.*
- Service dress is *less formal.*
- Business suit or tuxedo are also options.
- Enlisted personnel wear the corresponding uniform.

ARMY
- Mess blues are the *most formal.*
- Dress blues are appropriate for *less formal.*
- Enlisted personnel wear the corresponding uniform.

NAVY
- Dinner dress blues or summer whites are *most formal.*
- Service dress is worn for *less formal.*
- If there is an Arch of Sabers ceremony at a military wedding the bridegroom and attendants wear appropriate uniforms for the time of day or evening.

MARINES
- Evening dress for *most formal.*
- Blue dress or summer whites for less formal.
- Enlisted personnel wear blue dress or Service A uniforms for day or evening.
- Senior enlisted personnel have the option of wearing evening dress for *most formal,* Service A uniform for day wear, and blues for day or evening.

COAST GUARD
- Full dress summer whites or full dress blues for *most formal.*
- Service dress white or mess dress blues for *less formal.*

Military guests wear military attire appropriate for the branch in which they serve or they may wear civilian dress.

MILITARY CHAPEL WEDDINGS

A military wedding means the wedding takes place in the base chapel.

The regulations stipulate who may apply: those currently serving in the military and service retirees and their families. The Reserves and the National Guard have the use of chapels while serving on active duty.

There is no difference between a military and civilian wedding ceremony: Christians are married by chaplains of their own denomination, Jews by Jewish chaplains, and Hindus by Hindu priests. Chaplains of *all faiths* are bound by their religious orders as in civilian life but also by the regulations of the military organization in which they serve.

An application is made through the chaplain's office.

It is essential, as in civilian life, that as soon as the engagement takes place there be a meeting with the chaplain, who will ask the same questions a civilian clergyperson does—questions such as whether either has been married before, whether they are of the same denomination or religion and, if applicable, whether both have baptismal papers.

The chaplain also advises on the steps and requirements necessary for the preparation of a military wedding, such as medical tests, marriage license, the signing of the Marriage Register, and premarital marriage counseling.

Also, the chaplain sets the style of both the ceremony and processional. Any changes have to meet his or her approval.

It is not unusual to plan a year ahead for a military wedding. June is a popular month for marriages, especially at educational military sites, since it is graduation month.

There is no charge for the chapel. Reservations for it are on a first-come basis. Many wedding ceremonies take place on a given day—the time of day being determined by the luck of the draw.

Permission of the chaplain is needed if the hometown clergy-person is to assist in the wedding rites.

An active duty chaplain is paid by the military and will not accept a fee for officiating, but the visiting clergyperson or re-tired chaplain receives a fee. If the organist is also a member of the armed forces, there is no fee and the choice of music is from a prepared list. Civilian musicians are paid, as are other services such as a florist, wedding coordinator, and caterer.

A donation toward the upkeep of the chapel is fitting. The suggested donation, at the time of this writing, is around fifty dollars for the chapel. It is written out to the Chaplain Chapel Fund.

The bridal couple pays for the chapel decorations. However, since, at busy times, one wedding ceremony follows another, it might be impossible to have one's own preferences in floral arrangements. Also, it is the family's responsibility to leave the chapel clean and tidy for the next couple.

It is important that the base's security police be notified well in advance. They need the names and addresses of the guests and the time and dates of the rehearsal and wedding. Security directs your guests to the appropriate parking areas.

ARCH OF SWORDS (SABERS) CEREMONY

There are two reasons for the use of a sword. One is the cake cutting at the reception.

The other is the impressive Arch of Swords (Sabers) ceremony.

This ceremony is not a requirement, but if the couple wish one, it is their responsibility to arrange for it. An Arch of Swords (Sabers) ceremony is formed by an honor guard. It may take place indoors—with the permission of the chaplain—or out. The Army and Air Force conduct the saber ceremony in the same manner; the Navy has its own sword tradition, but the components are similar and the meaning is the same.

In a military wedding, an outdoor Arch of Swords ceremony takes place at the completion of the nuptial ceremony and after the recessional. The bride and bridegroom go into an anteroom to wait for the best man to announce that the officers have formed the arch.

Meanwhile, the attendants line up on either side of the chapel's main doors. Guests leave the chapel and stand on the steps on the grassy area or on either side of the steps. Six to eight uniformed officers, who may also have served as ushers, line up facing one another, swords in scabbards. Upon the command of the senior officer they draw swords in unison and raise them so the tips of the swords touch. The newlyweds pass under the arch and as they reach the end they stand for a moment. The head usher issues the command to sheathe swords. Waves of applause accompany the couple as they happily rush into the waiting limousine to take them to the reception.

The indoor Arch of Swords ceremony takes place just after the last blessing. The main difference is that the ushers line up along both sides of the aisle facing one another. When the bridal couple pass through, the sabers are returned to scabbards and only then do members of the bridal party continue with the recessional.

Double Wedding

Double weddings do not seem popular. Parents might have a joint engagement party and a joint engagement announcement in the paper, but one daughter has chosen a May date and the other wants to be a September bride.

But for those who choose a double wedding . . .

The tradition of the older bride being first in all phases of a double wedding dates back to biblical times when younger sisters could not marry until the eldest found a husband. For us it is an outdated notion, though still practiced in many countries. The custom for the double ceremonies seems a more orderly process.

The brides wear different-style dresses but the same length and formality. The clothing for all members of the wedding party is the same as for single weddings, so there might be some compromising on coordinating colors. It is best that each couple has the same number of attendants or even shares them. Brides may want to act as honor attendant for each other, and the bridegrooms may serve each other as best man. I think it less complicated when the two couples have their own honor attendants.

Double-wedding decisions must be carefully weighed by all sides and the expenses equally divided. I would think that there will be other sensitive aspects in the arrangements.

If you are contemplating a double wedding, consider the people involved—their tastes, style, and nature.

I like to think that over the years the couples will celebrate their anniversaries together.

Host Houses of Worship

There are houses of worship that accept those not directly connected with their institution—the Ethical Culture Society and the Unitarian Church, for instance. A telephone call will supply the information needed to arrange an appointment. The officiants will want to meet with the betrothed and go through counseling sessions as if the couple were members of the congregation.

Nevada is among the states where couples marry with little more than their physical presence. The couple reserve a private marriage chapel beforehand, apply at the marriage license bureau, and are issued a certificate within half an hour. The officiating minister, who is accommodating, and the couple meet to arrange the type of wording for the ceremony, be it secular

or religious. A small chapel is available if the couple is unac-
companied; there are larger chapels for wedding parties and
guests. A florist and photographer are available. Three weeks
later the newlyweds receive the license in the mail.

Civil Ceremony

Marrying in a civil ceremony answers a need for those who,
for various reasons, cannot or do not wish to go through a
religious ceremony.

Having obtained a marriage license, off to the courthouse
the couple go—the two of them, accompanied by two witnesses, or more if they wish. They stand before the officiant to
exchange vows and are pronounced husband and wife. It is a
private, quiet event involving few people. Some couples have
a big bash afterward. Others keep the reception low-key by
limiting the celebration to a wedding cake and champagne or
a luncheon for those who witnessed the ceremony.

Policies differ from state to state on who is allowed to perform civil marriage ceremonies. In some areas, only the Clerk
of the Court may do so; in others, judges, magistrates, and
public officials officiate. A telephone call to your county's marriage bureau service will determine that jurisdiction's policy.

After contemplating marriage for a while, a couple will suddenly decide that Friday the thirteenth is just the right time to
marry—perhaps it comes before a long weekend. So on Tues-
day he or she applies for a marriage license and on Friday they
appear at the registrar's office, ready for nuptial exchanges and
a three-day honeymoon.

Other couples have more complicated reasons—family in-
terference or different religious affiliations. It just makes it easier for the lovers to come home after the ceremony and
announce the fait accompli.

Having a civil ceremony does not preclude a religious ceremony of some sort. If the couple decide later to have a relig-

ious blessing of the marriage, they can ask their clergyperson for advice on the course to take.

Most religions have a "Blessing of the Marriage Service" without the exchange of rings or the bride being given away. The phrasing is similar to the formal marriage ceremony except that words such as "accept" are changed to "acknowledge."

Adherents of the Catholic and Greek (Eastern) Orthodox churches can have a full ceremony because a civil ceremony is not recognized by those churches.

Civil ceremonies are recognized in Jewish law.

In the United States, marrying in a civil ceremony meets the laws of the country. A religious wedding is also binding in the eyes of the law, since the officiant is licensed by the state to perform marriages.

In some other countries, such as France, the only recognized married state is that conferred in a civil ceremony. Most couples, after the civil exchange of vows, go right to the church and repeat the process according to its dictates. In England, most marriages take place within the Church of England.

If you are planning to marry overseas, check beforehand on the laws of the country. Most countries have a longer waiting period than in the United States and some have residency requirements.

The service starts with the words:

We are gathered here in the presence of these witnesses to join this man and this woman together in matrimony. The contract is a solemn one and not to be entered into lightly, but thoughtfully and seriously and with a deep realization of its obligations and responsibilities. If anyone can show just cause why they should not be lawfully joined together let him speak now, or else forever hold his peace.

———, will you take ———, here present, for your lawful wife [husband]?

I will.

I, _____, take you _____, for my lawful wife [husband], to have and to hold, from this day forward, for better, for worse, for richer, for poorer, in sickness and in health, until death do us part.

The exchange of rings is performed.

After the short ceremony, the couple is given a copy of the service, which ends . . .

By the power and authority vested by law as Clerk of the Circuit Court for Montgomery County, Maryland, I now pronounce you husband and wife.

Elopement

A marriage in secret, in either a civil or a religious ceremony, is considered an elopement. It is a legally binding union.

Questions about elopement center on what happens after the couple and family no longer want to keep the marriage a secret. If the newlyweds were married in a civil ceremony or by a clergyman, they may still want to have a service conducted by their own religious leader in the presence of their families.

Other areas of concern are whether announcements should go out after the wedding and, if so, is there a cut-off date.

Printed marriage announcements are sent to relatives, friends, and acquaintances. Newspaper notices are appropriate if they go out in a timely manner. Otherwise, it is old news.

The perennial question is whether to have a reception. Why not? Not only is it a practical way of introducing the newly-weds but also a way of welcoming the new spouse by family and friends.

The next inevitable query from those receiving announce-ments is whether they should send a present. Again, wedding announcements attach no obligation. The relationship to the couple and their families is the determining factor.

Intermarriage

"Tradition, tradition," sang the father in *Fiddler on the Roof.* But today's children are setting the stage for their own songs. Parents are having to look for clergy of different faiths who will co-officiate the exchange of marriage vows. Officiants are performing rites together, with each trying to retain the essence and beauty of their respective religions.

If ever we need to be sensitive to, and understanding of, one another, it is the day our child introduces a person of another denomination or faith and says: "We are going to marry." This is true for the young couple as well as for their respective parents, who need an understanding of the other side's beliefs and of their future in-laws' convictions.

It is important to define the meaning of the words "ecumenical" and "interfaith." "Ecumenical" refers to the mingling of Christian churches of different denominations. An "interfaith" service is a coming together of people of different faiths. Interracial marriages can be either ecumenical or interfaith unions.

Suppose the bridegroom's side of the family cares little about religious rites and the bride's family are deep believers. Arrangements with her family's clergyperson and place of worship should be virtually free of strain. But when both are strongly tied to their faiths, it becomes more complicated. The couple should have some knowledge of the religious marriage customs of the other.

Q: *My fiancé, an atheist, objects to being involved in a religious ceremony and feels that vows said in this fashion are without worth. I feel that unless the ceremony is performed by a man of the cloth the vows are not binding. We are very unhappy and do not know what to do.*

The obvious compromise would be that you have both a civil ceremony and a religious one. Another is to elicit the help of a clergyperson with the writing of your vows and incorporating what each of you considers of prime importance. Your love for each other will have to find a way.

Your differences, however, are serious because you both have strong beliefs. If one of you compromises totally now, it could spell trouble later in your marriage. The best chance a union has of succeeding is when two people share the same philosophy, which may not necessarily mean the same religion but the same values, goals, and outlook.

Though this book can guide you through a myriad of customs and wedding etiquette, deep philosophical differences require a knowledgeable marriage counselor or a religious adviser with experience in this area. If you don't feel free enough to go to your own clergyman, there are religious institutions that have counseling services. You may have to try more than one adviser—to find one who satisfies your needs and before whom you both can speak honestly.

Q: My fiancé is Jewish, and I am willing to be married by a rabbi, but we are having a hard time finding one who will perform the ceremony. Why do we have to say I am not Jewish?

You must be frank in your discussion with anyone you engage because it is unfair to religious leaders of all faiths to do otherwise. How will you answer questions without some background?

Most rabbis, whether Orthodox, Conservative, or Reform, will not perform the marriage ceremony if one of you is not Jewish. Though it is hard to find a rabbi who will officiate at an interfaith union, it is not impossible.

THE UNINVITED

Q: Do I have to pay for a wedding in which I will not be allowed to participate, or escort my daughter, or see her exchange marriage vows?

Oh, she must be marrying in the Mormon Church of Jesus Christ of Latter-Day Saints. The only people allowed in the temple itself are Mormons in good standing. Exclusion from the temple applies not only to those of a different faith but also to Mormons who have not met the standards set by the church.

What does your wife say about the position you are taking, and is your daughter being married in Utah?

Q: Our daughter is going to school in Utah. Her future husband's family lives there and are members in good standing. However, though my wife, a Mormon, isn't allowed to attend the ceremony, she still says I'm wrong. I should pay for the privilege of not being present at the marriage ceremony of our daughter. I feel they should change this ridiculous rule. After all, she is our daughter!

It's a strict rule, and there's nothing you can do. The rites don't take long. You wait in rooms at the Visitor's Center where a reception will take place. Also, since the exchange of wedding rings isn't part of the "sealing" rites, the couple may have an exchange-of-rings ceremony.

If you don't to go to Utah, you could honor the newlyweds at a reception, inviting your family, the young man's family, and friends to meet your daughter and her husband. Make it at a time when they may conveniently visit, even if you have to pay the airfare. This gesture would show caring and support. If you separate yourself from your daughter, it'll be difficult for her to approach you in the future should she need you, and you and your wife need her. I believe in open doors.

Your daughter may agree to a Blessing of the Marriage service. The Mormon Church has no objection, provided everyone understands that it can't be a full marriage ceremony. Check with your minister for permission.

KING SOLOMON AND THE CHILDREN

One young couple with different religious backgrounds settled a complicated question using King Solomon as a guide. The problem was: In whose religion would the children be brought up? They were unable to arrive at an agreement. So much in love, and with the wedding date fast approaching, they compromised by dividing the potential children in half; sons would go to their father's church and daughters would go to their mother's. I wondered what would happen if they had seven daughters, or seven sons. Would the parent with such a wealth of children share them with the other? He or she could generously say, "Look, I've got seven, today you can borrow Elizabeth and Joan (or John and William). . . ."

The Reception

Receiving Line—Bouquet Toss—
Order of the Garter

The menu for the reception after the wedding ceremony depends on the time of day or evening and whether the wedding is formal or informal. It also depends on the size of the guest list and where the function takes place—your home, the house of worship, a rented hall, a restaurant, or a hotel.

Eating is a habit humankind has developed over the past several million years, so you cannot expect your company to cure themselves of this malady on your wedding day. "Breaking bread" with one another brings warmth and fellowship. Its importance is documented in sacred books. Jesus at Cana performed his first miracle at the wedding feast by bringing forth wine from vessels of water. The Old Testament is filled with examples of the gathering of kinsmen to commemorate special events, especially weddings.

Try not to do more than you can afford, but be realistic. Consider the time of day the ceremony takes place and plan your reception accordingly.

If the ceremony takes place at eleven o'clock, serve some sort of brunch or luncheon. Lighter fare is acceptable if the exchange of vows is at two o'clock.

For the simplest of receptions you need a wedding cake, nuts, and mints. The traditional drink for toasting is champagne, but champagne punch and wine can be used, too. Also serve fruit punch or sparkling cider for people who do not drink other beverages, such as tea, coffee, wine, or liquor.

Most wedding receptions are buffet style. The food is placed on a long table, and the company helps themselves—a server might slice the roast beef, for example, as guests move through the line.

As guests enter the dining room, they pick up a place card with their name and table number on it. If the seating is informal, guests find places at available tables.

A stand-up reception can be tiring for those who find it hard to be on their feet for long periods of time. If possible, have chairs scattered about so that some relief is available; most guests rest a spell and then circulate, so it is unlikely you will need many.

The food arranged for a stand-up buffet reception should be easy to manipulate. Sliced meat on small rolls is manageable, but meat that has to be cut with a knife and fork while holding a drink in the other hand is nigh impossible for two-handed Homo sapiens.

After a morning ceremony, the menu might include fruit juice, quiche, omelets, and some sort of bread such as biscuits, muffins, or rolls and butter, along with coffee, tea, milk, a wedding cake, and champagne or champagne punch. Some people add fresh fruit.

Luncheon served after a noon ceremony runs the gamut from seafood to chicken to meat, salads, pasta, scones and rolls and butter, cookies; coffee, tea, and milk along with the wedding cake, a toasting drink, and ice cream. It can be served as a seated meal or a buffet.

An afternoon function might have all the aspects of a formal evening dinner and dance.

A simple afternoon tea, served between two and four o'clock, includes dainty finger sandwiches, petit fours (small iced cakes), tea, coffee, champagne, and wedding cake, nuts (or a mix of nuts and raisins), and mints. This menu is also customary in the Southwest for an evening wedding held at eight.

Sometimes an afternoon ceremony, held between two and five o'clock, is followed by a cocktail reception whose fare consists of hot and cold hors d'oeuvres, wedding cake, champagne, and wine, along with little cakes. Coffee and tea are optional. Another choice is the popular buffet luncheon.

A reception held at six o'clock or later suggests a more elaborate menu whether a supper, a buffet, or a served seated multiple-course meal. A lavish reception would include an "open bar" and hot and cold hors d'oeuvres during and after well-wishers leave the receiving line. It is followed by a served seated dinner with dancing and an open bar. Festivities extend into the night.

Make your decisions after you have calculated the entire cost for the various choices offered.

If you are having a home wedding, with good friends to help you with food preparation, chances are you can control your expenditure. However, you will have a great deal more responsibility. You can rent chairs, bridge tables, and accessories and put small vases of flowers on bridge cloths to go with your color scheme. You still need to rent little round cocktail tables and chairs, if the reception takes place elsewhere.

First, taking one area at a time, list what you will need other than food. Close your eyes and picture how you will serve the food from beginning to end.

- Plates—both the larger size for main dishes and smaller ones for dessert

Someone whispered in my ear that some caterers and hostesses use smaller plates to cut down on food consumption . . . Er, um, that is up to you.

- Forks and spoons—even if you are having finger food
- Utensils for the wedding cake
- Napkins—both dinner and cocktail size
- Champagne and liquor glasses
- Cups and saucers
- Cream pitchers and sugar bowls
- Serving trays

- Bowls and casserole holders with serving spoons and forks for each
- Punch bowls
- Chairs and tables, unless your guests are expected to stand

Most are rental items. I also recommend that you hire servers and a bartender.

Catering Services

The fact that weddings can become too complicated for mere mortals like me to cope with alone is one of the reasons why caterers and hotel banquet managers came into being. Their reputation is established by recommendations from satisfied customers and impressed guests.

Reputable professional caterers know their business and will have no hesitation about giving you telephone numbers of recent customers for you to speak to. Also caterers will invite you to taste the dishes being considered for the menu. Another source is your county's consumer affairs department, which you can call to find out whether there are any complaints registered about a firm you are considering.

Caterers prepare more food for a buffet meal than for a sit-down dinner, where guests are served a certain amount of food per person. Also, the latter is more expensive because more waiters are needed.

Drink to Me Only . . .

Liquor and champagne are expensive items. Professionals can guide you on the average amount guests consume, as they can with food. At one time hard liquor was popular, but wine and other liquids seem to have taken its place.

Because good champagne costs a lot more than table wine, an option for some is to have champagne at the bridal table for toasts, while guests are served wine—an acceptable practice. The estimate is four bottles of champagne for twenty-five people.

An open bar is also costly and requires a bartender. The open bar, which means that guests may order from a wide selection of hard liquor and wine, is available during the whole event or for only part of the time—perhaps while guests are going through the receiving line—while serving only wine during the dinner. Instruct the bartender on the time to close the bar.

The bartender should measure the standard amount of spirits because attitudes are changing on whether liquor should flow like water in a fountain. You do not want guests to go home tipsy, let alone drunk. A situation to be aware of: A mortified mother of the bride realized that the bartender was asking the guests to pay for their drinks; he had confused his instructions with another assignment! I hope it was the next job coming up and not the one before.

It is important to have on hand nonalcoholic drinks, such as soda and juice, for those who do not drink spirits.

In some parts of the country, a cash bar is acceptable. In olde England the bride's family had permission to sell ale at their daughter's wedding day to meet their expenses—hence the expression "bridal" (bride's ale), but unless it is a custom in your area do not consider it. Elsewhere, allowing guests to pay for anything at a wedding is considered improper.

If you are having a catered affair in a hotel, you pay for each bottle of liquor. Most establishments will not allow you to bring your own liquor, though if the wedding is large enough, say three hundred people, they might permit it, since money is made on the food. A friend of mine who was arranging her daughter's wedding reception at a hotel discussed with the maître d' the possibility of bringing her own champagne, wine, and wedding cake. He agreed to the wine and wedding cake but charged her per serving for cutting the cake and a bottle fee for opening and serving the wine. Even with the "corkage" fee, expenses were cut and she was able to have the brand she preferred. This is standard practice, but most people do not know about it. It is your responsibility to have the cake and wine delivered to the reception site.

Reception Services

Whether you engage a caterer for a home wedding or have a reception in a hotel, there will be a contract for you to sign. The banquet manager will go over the menu with you, giving you a choice of several; they are experts on how much food and drink you will need to cover the guest list. Some begin the conversation by asking how you envision your wedding reception and what type of food you prefer.

The manager will escort you through the banquet rooms and explain what the hotel's method of operation will be, enabling you to envision your reception within those walls. Make sure there are pleasant rest rooms and a checkroom for coats.

There is an important aspect to hiring services a year ahead. The costs quoted will be at *current* prices. The caterer must estimate that if there is an inflation period, there most likely will be an increase of 7 to 10 percent on the bill.

Keep a cool head. Some people feel intimidated at this time. The event is so important to them that they find it difficult to view the arrangements as a business deal, and a business deal it is with the professionals. It is an emotional and sentimental time. Just keep in mind that there are two perspectives—romantic and practical.

Paring costs and trying to get the best value for your money is sensible. Make an informed decision and then try for the best price you can. Some services have a small profit margin and a deal can be made within those limits, but that is not always a saving. A contractor has to have future dates on the books and may not want to refuse business, so be sure you are not running the risk of getting inferior services—chipped dishes, for instance. Your contract should say it all.

Ask if there are any *hidden charges* you should know about. Make it known that the fees quoted are what you expect to pay, other than the uncertain cost of food a year hence. An ethical business establishment will give you value for your money.

Take careful notes when discussing the various aspects of the reception. You may be speaking to a salesperson rather than to the manager, who then has to review the contract offered by sales. Changes might be made of which you are unaware until you receive the contract. Compare the contract with your notes. If there is a discrepancy, cross it out and initial each change. You must have your own copy of the contract.

After checking the date and time, the menu, prices, and services, the caterer or banquet manager will hold the wedding date for a specified number of days. If you are still uncertain after that period, you may lose the date to someone else. It is more likely that will happen if you choose a popular place in your area that has bookings as much as a year ahead. You can always ask for a short extension, but do so before the hold date elapses.

A few days after your visit, the firm will send a contract for you to sign and return by mail. Read it carefully. Check the wedding date and time of day first. See whether the contract agrees with your letter. If there is any discrepancy, do not hesitate to telephone the banquet manager. Reading from your letter, question the areas of doubt. Cross out the point of contention and write in the correction and initial it; both you and the caterer must initial. A sizable deposit is required, and once you sign the contract it is binding.

Wedding Cake

The wedding cake dates back to antiquity. During the wedding banquet, the ancient Greek bridal couple shared a sesame cake to ensure fertility. A bride and bridegroom, during the glory of Rome, started the wedding ceremony with a solemn offering to the officiant of a cake of spelt (a kind of wheat).

In the Middle Ages, guests crumbled little wheat cakes, also symbols of fertility, over the heads of the bridal couple. In some quarters, it guaranteed good luck for the bridegroom's mother to break bread over the bride's head as the new wife entered her home. In sixteenth-century England, a practical soul decided there was no point in wasting those tasty morsels and made little sugared cakes for consumption. Later, it was the French who imaginatively created the layered, iced wonder.

Nowadays the cake has its own unique character. Accompanied by a silver knife decorated with white bridal ribbon, it sometimes stands on the bride's table, or it can be placed alone or on a wheeled table.

Cakes can be the traditional pound or sponge cake layered with the usual fillings or creations of chocolate cakes with raspberry or even more exotic ingredients.

The bridegroom's cake is usually a chocolate or fruit cake that stands on the side of the bride's cake. Toward the end of the celebration, servers slice the cake and place the slices in small white boxes tied with white ribbons for guests to take as they leave. Or it can be served at the same time as the bride's cake.

There is a superstition that whispers to an unmarried girl that if she sleeps with the wedding cake under her pillow, she will dream of her own wedding, but there is no mention of the same thing happening to a hopeful bachelor—though it might work if you put the bridegroom's cake under the pillow. Gentlemen, try it! Who knows?

While the newlyweds slice the wedding cake, the band

softly plays the song chosen for their first dance as husband and wife. The bride stands on the bridegroom's right holding the knife as her husband places his hand on hers. She cuts a slice of cake from the bottom layer, which she and her husband share. Sometimes the first piece is sliced beforehand by a waiter to make it easier for the bride. Now waiters can divide the rest for guests.

At a military wedding, the bridegroom hands his sword to his new bride, who, with her husband's hand on hers, cuts the cake.

The top layer can be frozen. Discuss the best way to store your wedding cake with the baker, who knows the ingredients. Serve the cake, topped by the ornament that was originally on the confection, at the celebration of your first wedding anniversary—a sign of further good luck to the happily married couple. It is better than having it crumbled over your head.

Receptions After the Wedding Day

The reception that takes place on the wedding day is the wedding reception. Receptions held later are in honor of the newlyweds. The function may be formal or informal. The bride does not usually wear her wedding dress at a second reception. Having just written that sentence, I am reminded of an American girl who married in the States into a socially prominent British family. She told me she would wear her wedding dress and accessories to another ceremony in the chapel on his family's estate. His family, friends, and neighbors, who were unable to make the trip to America, will be present.

There may be special reasons for wearing the wedding dress again, but it does not seem suitable to wear the costume at a reception. If you feel that guests would like to see the bridal ensemble, display it in the reception room.

Oft times, his family will have a reception for the honeymooners in his hometown, when distance prevented the bridegroom's people from attending the wedding.

Seating

BRIDAL TABLE

The bride and bridegroom sit facing the company at the center of an oblong or semicircular table. The bride is on the bridegroom's right, the best man on her right; the honor attendant sits on the bridegroom's left; next to the maid of honor is an usher; then a bridesmaid, and so on.

PARENTS' TABLE

It depends on the number of people whether there are two separate tables for the parents and close honored guests.

When all sit at one table, the arrangements are the same as at any social occasion. The bride's parents, the host and hostess, sit across from each other. The father of the bridegroom sits on the right of the hostess and to her left is the officiant. The bridegroom's mother is on the right of the host, whose left-hand guest is the officiant's spouse. Since tables at a hotel seat from eight to ten, there is room for four more at the table. Of course, grandparents—as honored guests—would be the first choice. Other close relatives might warrant the honor if there were no grandparents or officiant present.

Some couples decide that their parents will sit with them at the bride's table. Attendants, unless there is room, sit with the rest of the company. At a long oval table, the bridal couple sit together in the middle of one side, with the host at one end and the hostess at the other. The bridegroom's parents and the clergyperson and spouse sit as explained above. Another choice is a round table for the bride and bridegroom to sit at alone facing the guests.

The seating arrangement at some ethnic weddings has the bride's family and intimates at one table and the bridegroom's family and their honored guests at a table opposite.

Tables and chairs are used at a buffet reception, and the formation is the same as with a dinner reception. However, even if there is sparse random seating or only a few chairs for guests, there should be a table for the bride and bridegroom.

The "honeymoon table" is a small round table seating only the bride and bridegroom, who have their first meal together as husband and wife. It avoids problems such as what to do with divorced parents at the bridal table and who sits with the bride and bridegroom. They may prefer it that way simply because they wish to circulate among the guests and dance.

At a less-formal buffet reception the bridal couple might choose not to have a separate table but to circulate among their guests and eat at will.

GUEST SEATING

Ah, if you can seat all your guests so that they live happily ever afterward with the knowledge that they are special to you, you will be awarded the prize of diplomat of the year—especially if half the guests are not speaking to the other half.

Calm down, it is not as serious a chore as that, but a word of caution: Never try to mediate disputes by seating estranged people together. It might work out so well that you will be voted a champion, but it might backfire, too. Also, it is almost impossible to seat all your friends or all of one side of the family together. As long as you do not seat an adult couple at a children's table—I'm not kidding!—because you had only a certain number of tables and very few children, *or* due to last-minute cancellations you had to rearrange the tables and it had nothing to do with the couple but that particular place card had fallen off the table and it was three o'clock in the morning . . . See what I mean?

Too few children? Seat them with their parents. A couple or two who do not know anyone at the wedding other than their hosts? Seat them at a table with people who are hospitable, even if you have to move one or two couples from that table who are close to the others. Your guests do not expect, nor should they, to be seated as if they were invited to a small dinner party in your home. Mix groups, but with discretion. A couple in their thirties are not seated at a table with the bride's elderly great-aunts, to listen to how things were when ladies wore gloves and hats and men held doors open for them.

PLACE OR ASSIGNMENT CARDS

When you ordered the invitations, etc., you were advised, I hope, to pick up table assignment cards that are used at large weddings to show guests where they are supposed to sit.

For a formal wedding, write the guests' names by hand on each assignment card: Mr. and Mrs. Wilson; Dr. and Mrs.; Rev. and Mrs., without first names—unless there is more than one couple with the same last name. Single people are also addressed by their surnames: Mr. Friendly, Miss Charming, or Ms. Sophisticated. Couples living together would still have individual place cards or one name below the other. It is inappropriate to designate a dignitary with "the Honorable." Use the person's actual title—Governor and Mrs., or Justice and Mrs., for instance—or revert to Mr., Mrs., or Ms. when appropriate.

At smaller, more intimate gatherings, the bride and bridegroom use the names they usually call their relatives and friends on the place cards.

TABLE ASSIGNMENTS

To plan table assignments, count the acceptances, then consult the banquet manager about the number of tables needed. Now the job is almost completed.

Take a large sheet of paper. Draw as many circles as there are tables. Arrange the place cards into compatible groups around the circles; some tables can hold eight and others ten. Move the cards as if they were chess pieces until the right combinations are achieved. Check the carpet for stray cards and count heads. Be sure to put the correct table number on each place card. You would not want an extra couple standing about wondering why there is no room at the table they were assigned.

Receiving Line

"Feliciter—may happiness await you!" was the response of ancient Romans after the wedding ceremony.

The choice of holding the receiving line after the ceremony at the house of worship, or afterward at the reception site, is optional. It is particularly true if everyone is invited to both the ceremony and reception. If many came to the ceremony but not to the reception afterward, they will appreciate being able to express their wishes for the couple's happy future before leaving. Then, of course, a line at the reception is unnecessary. Either way, it is a happy time.

Just picture it. The ceremony was perfect. The drive to the reception gave the couple a little time to be by themselves, and the photographer has taken the necessary photographs of the bridal party. Now the festivities are about to begin. . . .

Closest to the entrance to the reception room is the bride's mother (or hostess), who receives well-wishers and presents them to the bridegroom's mother. Guests go down the line to greet the bride and bridegroom, who briefly introduce to each other those people they may not yet have met. They spend only a few moments with each person, and that enables the line to move quickly.

Why do some people find receiving lines a nuisance? Why, I am asked, do I have to have a receiving line? They are so tiresome; after all, some Jewish weddings do not have receiving lines. The bride and bridegroom see to it that they visit every table and parents make their rounds also.

I know, I know, but if handled correctly the receiving line is practical. It is an orderly process and avoids the confusion bridal couples sometimes face when they are surrounded by guests wishing them well. I venture to whisper in your ear that it relieves both guests and the bridal couple of saying more than a few well-chosen words of good wishes and thank-yous.

To speed up the line have an usher, a relative perhaps, to discreetly guide people to the refreshments. Sometimes there is a waiter nearby with a tray of drinks or finger food to lure guests in the right direction.

If the receiving line takes place at the house of worship, it is formed in the vestibule. Conversation is likely to be less inviting there, so the line moves faster.

At a home reception, when the ceremony has taken place at the house of worship, the hostess and the bridegroom's mother stand near the door welcoming the company. The bride and bridegroom have a word with each guest as they come near.

Q: Until now, I've had no objection to going through a receiving line, but, as the bride, I'm petrified that I won't remember anyone's name —not even my own. Any tips?

My self-conscious friend, are you too young to remember movies of grand balls where the butler stands, terribly correct, calling out in a clear, resonant voice the name of each guest so that the host and hostess are saved the embarrassment of not remembering them?

Try to keep your perspective and poise. On the most important day of your life, it is understandable that you may not recall everyone's name.

Guests should introduce themselves or say something that will give you a clue as they approach you and your husband. However, you are expected to recognize your mother, father, brothers, and sisters, some relatives, and a friend or two, and it is very good form to include your mother- and father-in-law.

A comforting thought—you are working with the names on the invitations and on table seating as well as writing thank-you notes, so you will not be as inept as you think.

ORDER OF RECEIVING LINE

GUIDELINES

The receiving line has many permutations, so you have choices. It depends on how long or short you wish it.

Below is the traditional receiving line:

- Mother of the bride
- Father of the bridegroom (optional)
- Bride and bridegroom
- Mother of the bridegroom
- Father of the bride (optional)
- Matron of Honor
- Maid of Honor
- Bridesmaids

The best man and the ushers generally do not stand in the line—they mingle with the guests.

For a shorter line, release the bridesmaids to join the guests. Fathers also circulate among the guests and occasionally join the line.

The bride, still holding her bouquet, stands on the right of the bridegroom for both civilian and armed-forces weddings. She may wear gloves (if they are part of her ensemble), but guests do not.

The place chosen for the receiving line should not hamper the easy flow of people from the entrance to the refreshments.

Guests going through the receiving line should offer brief remarks. This is no time to ask whom the newlyweds are voting for.

Handshakes should be firm, neither wrist breaking nor too weak.

The receiving line is over when all the guests have arrived and made their way down the line.

The guest book is on a table not far from the end of the receiving line. An attendant asks guests to sign the book. Only one of a married couple need sign for both: "Mr. and Mrs. Joseph Doe," or "Joseph and Virginia Doe."

DIVORCED PARENTS AND THE RECEIVING LINE

As with any social event, it is the hosts who receive.

If the bride's father and his current wife are hosting the reception, they head the receiving line. The bride's mother mingles with the guests.

If neither parent has remarried but they are sharing expenses, the bride's mother receives.

If the father is hosting the reception, his mother or his close relative does the honors, unless he wants to do so himself.

If the mother of the bride has remarried and she and her husband are responsible for the reception, she receives alone or with her husband.

However, when the receiving line takes place after the ceremony in a house of worship or at a site away from the reception hall, the bride's mother heads the line, no matter who is hosting the reception. Sometimes the vestibule is too small to have more than the mother of the bride, the bride and bridegroom, and the mother of the bridegroom.

At a small or a home wedding ceremony, the bridal couple turns to the company after the ceremony to receive well-wishers.

SUBSTITUTE HOSTS

If the bride's mother has passed away, her father stands in the receiving line. If both are deceased, ask a close relative. Though it is helpful to the bridal couple to have someone stand first in line, they might feel that they can manage on their own.

DOUBLE WEDDING RECEIVING LINE

If the brides are sisters, form one receiving line. There are two lines when the brides are friends, since there are two sets of hosts and separate families involved. Again, there are a number of permutations that the families can work out for a smooth receiving line.

GUIDELINES
- Mother of the brides
- Mother of older bridegroom
- Older bride
- Older bridegroom
- Younger bride
- Younger bridegroom
- Mother of younger bridegroom
- Older bride's honor attendant
- Younger bride's honor attendant

If the fathers of the bridegrooms stand in line, the father of the older bridegroom places himself on the left of his wife. The bridal couples stand next to each other. The younger bride-groom's parents stand to their son's left.

FRETFUL EX

Q: My ex-husband is paying for the entire wedding. He and his wife are going to head the receiving line as host and hostess. My daughter is upset because she was told I won't be on the receiving line also. Is she right?

Though only the hosts stand on the line and the ex-wife is a guest, some families do invite the divorced mother to join the line. They reason that she belongs there, though she is further down the line. Everyone knows who the hosts are—they are heading the line.

It depends on the grace of your ex and his wife. Your daughter would have to approach her father, not you. If he is adamant, reassure your daughter that you don't mind.

Ladies and Gentlemen, I have repeatedly read that weddings are different from any other social occasion, so I cannot understand omitting the natural parents from the receiving line, unless there is a real reason. Are not the relatives and friends of the bride's mother there to extend the same wishes to her as other members of the family are receiving, to say nothing of her daughter's new family?

I call on you, Ladies and Gentlemen, to right a wrong.

QUARRELSOME FATHER

Q: I am just checking about wedding protocol of divorced parents before I start planning my wedding. My father is paying for the entire wedding. He wants to sit in the first pew with his wife and have my mother sit in the third. Also, he doesn't want her in the receiving line.

Ladies and Gentlemen, that is not nice.

I outlined the rules to the young lady, adding that she do a little research in the library and show the suggested etiquette to him. Her father might change his mind when he realizes that it will show him and possibly his current wife to no good advantage if he insists on usurping his ex-wife's rightful place in *church*. She, herself, should not mention the receiving line.

RECEIVING-LINE EXEMPTIONS

Every able body should go down the receiving line, but it is particularly hard for some people to wade through a long receiving line, especially citizens of the third stage (senior citizens), as the British say. They can forgo it or the hostess can assign an usher to take them to the front of the line. The offer is made discreetly, since it could be declined. To a twenty-year-old, a graying fifty-year-old may seem ancient, nor would one want to insult a vigorous seventy-five-year-old man by treating him as if he were infirm.

Q: I am the elderly woman who has called you many times over the past few years. I try not to be too much of a stickler for the "correct thing," but nowadays younger people don't seem to be conscious of some of the niceties that go into making life a little more gracious.

Remember I called you when new neighbors moved in and I wanted to leave my calling card as a friendly gesture? Well, I followed your advice by taking a plate of cookies and putting my calling card on top. It worked out fine.

Now I am invited to their wedding. Why they're having a big wedding when they've been living together for quite some time I can't figure out. As I've explained to you before, though the bride is successful in her career, she doesn't know the first thing about protocol or etiquette. She seems to use intuition, which doesn't always work, so I've been helping her with wedding arrangements and again everything is working out fine.

I've just been to the doctor and he tells me that my heart is not strong. I will be attending the wedding next week, but I shall not be up to going through the receiving line. Yet I don't feel comfortable about not doing so. How shall I handle it?

Mrs. Que, of course I remember you. Some of your questions are laced throughout the book I am writing on wedding etiquette. This one about the receiving line and infirm people is very interesting.

Chances are the bridal couple won't realize you didn't make the receiving line, because people become a sea of faces to them after a while. Just skip the line and find a seat for yourself until it is over. Then you'll have the strength to join in the festivities. During the reception, when the bridal couple make their rounds, you'll have your moment with them.

POSTSCRIPT

Mrs. Que was kind enough to call me after the wedding, which she said was just wonderful. The bride and bridegroom, who hosted the wedding, stood at the entrance of the room welcoming guests assisted by their parents. Mrs. Que was greeted with great warmth, and thanks came not only from the bridal couple but from her mother for all the guidance she had given the couple during the past few months.

Mrs. Que: I was surprised that there was no receiving line.

Small weddings really don't require a line.

Mrs. Que: Maybe not. Anyway, I really had a good time and I did wear the diamond pin on my dress as you suggested. But I did something really awful—the wine must have been strong, though I only had a little, I'm not used to it.

What happened?

Mrs. Que: The music was so lively and I was having a lovely time. I went over to the drummer and talked to him. You know that is just not done. I feel so foolish.

Compliments are music to a performer's ears.

Dancing

According to wedding etiquette, no one dances with the bride until she and her bridegroom have had their first dance together. It does not mean, as some have told me, that dancing *only* takes place after the bride and bridegroom open the dancing. The party celebrating the marriage begins with the receiving line and if the band is playing, guests dance.

The music starts while the receiving line is being formed outside the reception room. For a smooth transition from the ceremony to the reception, musicians set up early so that the strains of music float from the reception room to the receiving line.

Before a seated dinner there might be a cocktail reception and a bartender serving drinks. People mingle, renewing old acquaintances and touching base with family they have not seen in ages. Others like to dance, while other guests find their seats at appointed tables.

Some bridal couples choose to open the dancing as soon as the receiving line is over. The maestro plays their favorite tune while the guests clear the floor and enthusiastically welcome the new Mr. and Mrs. Hampenstance. As with any function, the guests' primary duty is to make the celebration a successful one by participating.

Train swept up over her left arm, a move she practiced earlier in front of a mirror, the bride is led by the bridegroom into the type of dance they both feel comfortable with. But one hopes that they can glide into a melody reflecting the romantic mood of the occasion, leaving the faster music until later.

The choice of when the bridal dance takes place is a personal matter, as is the order of partners who dance with the bride during this special custom. It can take place at the cocktail reception, or some prefer it after or before dessert at a seated dinner. However, sometimes people do not feel comfortable about dancing without the bridal couple's participation, so guests will not have much of a chance to dance with the bride or bridegroom when the bridal dance takes place after the dessert.

Dancing may take place between courses, even if the bridal couple has not yet danced together.

Once bride and bridegroom now have circled their way around the dance floor for their first dance together, the traditional formal procedure for the bridal party to follow is:

- After a few turns with her father-in-law, the bride dances with her father.
- Then the best man asks the bride to dance.
- Meanwhile the bridegroom dances first with his mother-in-law, next with his own mother, and then with the honor attendant.
- The bride's father, after dancing with his daughter, invites the bridegroom's mother to dance, while the bride's father whirls his new son-in-law's mother around.
- Parents of the bridal couple dance with one another.
- The head usher dances with the bride while the best man and honor attendant pair off.
- Meanwhile, ushers and maids join in. Then guests fill the dance floor.
- Ushers and male guests dance once with the bride.

Naturally, divorced parents dance with their children and with their children's in-laws. If feelings are still awkward, children should not expect parents to dance with each other, despite the desire to see parents together for just one more time. Insisting might hurt one or both parents.

There is a more dramatic way for the newlyweds to enter the dining room. The bridal party moves out of sight once the receiving line is over. When guests take their places in the dining room, there is a gentle rolling of the drum to signal the entrance of the attendants. Couple by couple, as they are introduced by the band leader, they form an aisle for the bridal couple to move swiftly through to the bridal table while the standing company applauds.

Once the bridal dance is over, the music takes on its own special tone, from American swing, jazz, pop, country live dancing, R&B, Motown, or rock. The list includes dance rituals based on "Old World" traditions: the graceful Greek Misirlu, lively Polish polkas, Irish jigs, Highland flings, Virginia reels, Mexican hat dances, the Jewish horas, and Italian tarantellas.

The hora, which is played at most Jewish weddings, is the type of dance that allows for no wallflowers in the room, for every able body joins in. All form a gigantic circle, surrounding the happy pair, or a semicircle, so that the line weaves its way around the dance floor while nimble feet do the traditional steps.

One custom increasing in popularity at Jewish weddings is the carrying of the bride and bridegroom on chairs. Four strong "joyful" men place the bride in a chair. Four strong "joyful" men place the bridegroom in another chair. They lift the chairs with their precious cargo and carry them around the dance floor. Meanwhile the music plays and the crowd cheers. With nervous grins, the bride and bridegroom hold on for dear life to the sides of their chairs. One of my sources of amusing stories tells me that he played at one wedding in which the bridegroom was carried in a folding chair—the rest I leave to your imagination.

By the way, this spontaneous happening is hard to control

once it begins and cannot be controlled by the band leader. If the couple want to forgo the ride high above the company, they should make their wishes known to the best man and their respective families beforehand.

Toasts

Most bridal couples prefer that the toast take place after dessert and before the cake cutting.

Traditionally, the best man proposes the first toast. The company stand and raise glasses to the newlyweds. The bridal couple remain seated but refrain from lifting their glasses because those being toasted do not drink to themselves.

Rising to his feet, the bridegroom replies, combining a toast to his bride and thanks to both her parents and his. Then the bride toasts her husband and both sets of parents. Sometimes fathers or mothers feel moved to follow, but if there was toasting at the rehearsal dinner, they would have made their pronouncements at that time.

The Bouquet Toss
and the Order of the Garter

There are certain events that some weddings incorporate but of which other couples will have no part. Guess which of these two routines the soul of a shy or independent nature would find trying.

BOUQUET TOSS

The bride tosses the bouquet and the bridegroom retrieves the garter from the bride's leg toward the closing of the wedding celebration. All single girls are encouraged to try to catch the bouquet, for rumor has it that the nimble damsel will be the next to marry.

A raised area such as a staircase or balcony is an ideal place for the bouquet toss, but most of the time the bride throws it from the middle of the dance floor, where the band leader can maintain contact with the action. The bride can either turn her back to the audience and throw the bouquet over her shoulder, or face the maidens directly, which would give her a truer aim.

Simple event? Seems so! But there have been occasions when the bouquet has come apart while tossed into the air, showering its contents on the delighted crowd, or thrown so erratically that it landed in the aisle. One place in the Washington area has a balcony just for throwing the bouquet. The bride and bridegroom stand above the crowd, and all applaud the toss. However, more than one bride turned her back on the crowd, tossed the bouquet too high, and it landed in the chandelier. The teller of these stories says that invariably a Sir Lancelot stands on a chair attempting to grab the wayward prize while simultaneously looking up and down trying to keep his balance.

ORDER OF THE GARTER

The garter is said to be a substitute for the ribbon which the lady presented her champion knight of King Arthur's Round Table who gallantly carried her colors into battle. The Order of the Garter was formed in England in the fourteenth century, as an honor given to distinguished noblemen, who to this day wear a heraldic garter as part of their ceremonial garb. Having said that, I ask you to please read our answer to the British Crown. . . .

With the aid of the band, which plays a seductive tune, the bride sits on a chair while guests gather around. The bridegroom, on his knees, reaches for the garter, which the bride has placed just below her knee—any higher is considered provocative. Slowly, and with great deliberation, he slides the frilly blue elastic down the owner's leg. All the bachelors gather while the bridegroom, back to the audience, tosses the garter to them. The lucky catcher, who it is said will be the next married man (sorry, chaps . . . again, 'tis written in countless books on wedding superstitions) is then required to put the garter on the leg of the lady who caught the bouquet—every inch above the knee equals five years of happiness for the bridal couple.

Again, simple? Seems so! However, this is the time for a treatise on the garter—a reminder of the loss of innocence—written expressly for the dear bridegroom. This portion of my book is highly educational. . . .

Since the garter is of thin elastic, it is virtually weightless and cannot be thrown with momentum. To give the throw more force, ball the garter so that it can carry in the air until it unfolds and lands where you wish it to. Some swains, and I do not mean you, sir, throw it unenthusiastically, or before the signal from the band leader, so that it falls limply to the ground when no one is watching. Now the bridegroom has failed in this Olympian task and refuses do it again—that might be a great relief to the potential catcher, since a precocious eleven-year-old pre-damsel has caught the bridal bouquet. However, the band leader, photographer, and company are waiting for the lark to be completed, and the gentleman just has to rise to the occasion once again.

A word of caution: Watch out for the newly engaged gentleman whose fiancée has caught the bouquet. I know a young man who did leapfrogs over the other contenders, for he certainly was not going to allow anyone else's eager young hands to put that garter on his lady love.

BIRTH CERTIFICATE, PLEASE

Q: Is there an age limit on catching the bride's bouquet? At a wedding I attended recently, the young ladies gathered before the bride for the bouquet toss. A sixty-year-old widow rushed in front of them to join in the catch. Would you believe she caught it? Everyone sort of laughed, but I wonder about the appropriateness of it.

Well, though admittedly not a girl, she was single. It sounds to me as if Mrs. Bouquet Catcher decided impulsively to be part of the singles scene.

Appropriate? On the one hand, the bouquet and garter tosses are supposed to be fun and not taken seriously. On the other hand, the widow was at a distinct advantage over her opponents. On the other hand of the other hand, age has its benefits. What young girl would try to trip her for the prize?

(When a friend read these last two sentences, she said: "Oh, yeah!")

Q: What about the twenty-year-old man who caught the garter? Though he carried it off well enough, he couldn't have been too happy; he had the good sense to stop at the calf of her leg.

That was good judgment on his part, as it was when an eleven-year-old caught the bouquet, and the young gentleman just put the garter around her ankle. There is a thin line between fooling and foolish.

Ladies and Gentlemen, after the gathering of the maidens for tossing of the bouquet, one band leader was heard to ask the bride whether there were any shrinking violets in the room who should be joining in the ritual. The new matron offered her mom who, thinking to herself, "and I gave birth to this child," was caught sneaking out of the room along with two or three cousins of the unattached persuasion. Oh, well, it's all part of the game.

Taking Leave

Leavetaking has no set pattern.

The bridal couple might stay and close the festivities with a final dance to the music played for their first dance. The bride also dances with her father and the bridegroom dances with his mother.

The newlyweds might take their leave after the bouquet-garter toss if they are starting for their wedding trip from the reception. Their parents leave the guests for a short while to bid the children a private adieu and at that time they might present their parents with a small gift of thanks.

If it is a daytime wedding, the best man signals everyone to gather outdoors to form an aisle for the happy pair. Cheering them on to the car, the company throws birdseed, or whatever is the current environmental trend. The party can continue, but chances are it has wound down by then.

Some couples stay in the area until all out-of-town guests have left. When family and friends come from afar, or if the newlyweds live elsewhere, they might want to extend the visit another day before going on their wedding trip.

As Roman bridal couples were wished:

Feliciter—may happiness await you.

Second
Wedding and
Divorce

2uestions on second weddings and divorce overlap somewhat, so I have included both topics in this chapter. Second-wedding questions generally start with happy ones on procedure. Those on divorce are more complicated and often involve entire families including the divorced spouse. So, this chapter falls into two parts.

Second Wedding

When a couple plans a second wedding, they want to know what the guidelines are.

A bride with a conservative outlook may choose a simple wedding ceremony in a house of worship, the clergyman's office, or at home.

Send handwritten letters or telephone invitations to fifty or fewer guests. The bridal couple have one attendant each.

The bridegroom wears a business suit and the bride a street-length suit or dress.

Her father, a close relative, or a friend escorts her, or she can walk alone behind her honor attendant. The giving-away part of the ceremony is dispensed with.

A wedding breakfast or a luncheon follows or, if desired, a gala reception takes place anytime with as many guests as desired.

However, though the couple's wishes may be very simple, there are variations in approach to a second wedding that can still be within the bounds of what they consider good taste.

Weddings have not changed much over the last hundred years. There have been variations in style but in the basic ceremony the bridal couple still exchange vows, whether they write them themselves or use the traditional wording.

What has changed is the attitude of some second-time-around brides who want a traditional wedding, including the bridal gown and headdress—though no veil. A son may be ring bearer and a daughter the maid of honor. The affair from beginning to end has all the trimmings of the first time, though the bride and her future husband may foot the bill.

Etiquette specialists faced a crisis that began toward the end of the nineteen sixties. Young men and women were questioning every aspect of the rules of protocol and etiquette, an attitude that seemed out of control to parents and the experts.

Gradually, some of the traditions were relaxed because there was no choice in the matter. Also, gradually, toward the end of the seventies, I began receiving an influx of telephone calls increasingly on wedding-related protocol and etiquette issues that reflected, for some, a going back to basics but certainly not completely.

Q: *Is it incorrect for my parents to issue the invitations to my formal wedding? My friends tell me that a woman in her thirties who has been married before issues her own invitations.*

Your parents certainly may do the honors.

Q: *I am helping arrange the wedding of a forty-year-old woman and a man of sixty—a businessman of substance and highly respected in the community. I've tried to guide the bride about what type of function is suitable for a mature couple who have been married before. But the bride, the mother of two teenage children, is going to wear a traditional wedding dress, and the groom will be in formal attire to go with her outfit. She insists that it's what she wants and he says whatever she wants is the way it'll be. They're like two young kids. I'm debating whether to continue handling the affair.*

I see no reason to withdraw your services. The type of wedding the bridal couple wants will not be unusual to the guests. All you can do is to offer your advice, which they are free to accept or not, and your services for the making of a successful and smooth wedding.

It is not easy to meet a person whom one wants to marry, and most people are lonely before finding that special someone. When they do, happiness brims over with the wonder of it all. I see nothing wrong with it. It's like finding one's youth.

Ladies and Gentlemen, I think that I received the announcement of that wedding, along with a splendid photograph of the couple. It was the bride herself who handled the details of the newspaper announcement, not the bridal consultant. The photograph was of a slim, lovely woman in her forties gowned in a Victorian-style dress and picture hat. She held the arm of her husband, who was a head taller. His graying Vandyke beard and traditional formal attire completed the overall elegance of the photograph. The announcement listed the participation of their children in the wedding ceremony.

TAKING SIDES¿

Q: I am a bridal consultant whose clients are discussing having an engagement announcement in the newspaper. The future groom wants one very much since it is his first marriage. However, the bride has been married before and wants to know if it would be in good taste to have one. Also, she wants her eighteen-year-old daughter to be the maid of honor, but the groom says it shows the daughter is taking sides. I am not sure how to answer that.

Taking sides¿ Does the bridegroom mean the bride's daughter is taking the side of her mother against her father if she is her mother's maid of honor¿

Q: Yes, I guess so, but I am not sure.

The role her daughter is undertaking has to do with the wedding itself. I don't see it as a rejection of her father, who would receive the same support from her, but rather a problem with the bridegroom—a hidden concern. The young lady shouldn't even discuss it with her father. What if he disapproves and puts her in an unenviable position—squarely between her mother and father.

The answer to the couple's first question is to place a forthcoming marriage announcement:

Jill Candace Ode and Frederick Eldon Hampenstance are engaged to be married in the spring . . . [etc.]

The rest of the story may include the backgrounds of the forthcoming bride and bridegroom, including their parents.

ONCE IS ENOUGH

The parents hosted an expensive traditional wedding for their daughter. Now she is divorced, and though her parents are happy their daughter is marrying again, they are not in the same financial position to do anything elaborate. What do other parents do, her mother asks?

When money is no problem, they host another wedding, and some of those weddings are as elaborate as the first.

Some parents give their daughter the amount of money they can afford and the rest is up to the bridal couple. One large wedding per child is the formula.

This question has a different twist. It is from a mother whose divorced daughter and her fiancé are hosting their own wedding. However, her mother questions her daughter's wish for a traditional wedding. Moreover, her mother feels uncomfortable about the children being part of the wedding party: "It was so different when I was young and dealing with conflicts, and even shame, about my parents and divorce. Are children of this generation so advanced that they can think and feel like adults? They are only six and nine years old."

Children are more sophisticated today than at any time in recent history. They have to deal with problems of development and possess knowledge that in the past would have been considered beyond a child's ken.

Today's approach is to make the children part of the process—if they can handle it—so that they do not feel left out. Help them see the ceremony as a solemn service. There are children, however, who resist taking an active part in the ceremony.

Surely, I said to the caller, you would not want them to experience their mummy or daddy coming home with a new spouse, saying: "Darlings, we're married! Isn't that fun?"

A great deal depends on the individual child. If the child's natural parent is recently deceased, someone close should be standing by.

GRANDPARENTS, WIDOWS, AND CHILDREN

Divorce is not the only hurtful happening with which people have to contend. Widows and widowers with children, and the children themselves, whether young or adult, have to cope with a permanent separation not of their own choosing. Trying to build a new relationship and a new life and getting others to accept the change is tough.

Q: I'm a widow with two young children, and I'm planning to re-marry. My late husband's parents have been close to my children and me. Do I invite them to the wedding? I didn't expect to feel so upset about it, and I do not want to hurt them.

Discuss your feelings openly and honestly with your in-laws. After all, not only have you been a loving daughter-in-law and they loving in-laws, but you share the same bereavement—though on different levels. They may not resent, and may even be happy, that you're building a new life. However, I would imagine it painful for them to witness the process. If you are comfortable about it, leave the decision up to them.

Much depends on the type of man you're marrying and the way you set the pattern of your new life with him. This person will have a great influence on their grandchildren. If he has parents of his own, the children's grandparents may fear they'll be pushed aside. They'll need reassurance that their grandchildren will still be part of their lives, and rightly so. The grandparents may have accepted their loss, but it is still a constant source of pain. Those children are not only a joy to them but represent a continuity that we all hope for.

It'll be a rich experience for the children in their growing years to have loving people around them, but it will hurt to be alienated from their natural grandparents and will amount to another painful separation.

REMARRIAGE GUIDELINES

- It is inappropriate to have an announcement if one or the other is still married, no matter how thrilled the couple are with each other.
- Elopement is a legal marriage and so is a civil ceremony.
- Being free to marry means that both have gone through the process of divorce and have legal papers from the state to prove it.
- If an annulment took place, meaning that it is as if the first marriage never occurred, the annulment documents should be shown to the other partner.
- In addition to civil divorce, some religions—the Roman Catholic and the Eastern Orthodox churches, for instance

—require a religious divorce under their auspices in order to marry again within that denomination. Advice of clergy should be sought.

- Some religions do not permit remarriage while the ex-partner is still living. They may, however, sanction a service of marriage after a civil ceremony.
- According to Jewish law, which is observed by all Orthodox and most Conservative congregations, a Jewish divorce, called a "get," is required. Gets are issued by rabbis, who have the authority to grant them, and their decisions have to be within prescribed rabbinical law.

 There is one part of the Jewish divorce law that women consider unfair. A woman cannot obtain a divorce on her own behalf without her husband's permission, though he can divorce her at will. Also, he can withhold the divorce until he wishes to remarry—only then is she free to marry.

 Many Conservative couples add to the marriage contract (*ketubah*) the provision that should a civil divorce occur, a Jewish divorce can be petitioned by either party.

- When a widow or widower remarries, his or her deceased spouse's family should be notified of the impending marriage by letter or telephone, if there has been a drift away from the spouse's family.
- A widow generally wears her wedding ring until she remarries.
- A divorcée has a choice, sometimes choosing to wear the ring on her right hand or not wear it at all.
- Even if the marriage lasts only a short time, whether through death or divorce, wedding presents are not returned.
- Presents for a second marriage from those who gave the first time are not obligatory, but family and friends generally do give gifts.
- If presents are unwanted, family and friends should spread

the word, or write "no gifts, please" on a separate slip of paper and include it in the envelope.

- Traditionally, a widow uses her deceased husband's name:

  "Mrs. James Person Ode."

  Again, traditionally, when remarrying she would assume her new husband's name.

- Today divorcées have the choice of using their given names and their former husband's surname: Mrs. or Ms. Sarah Manning Ode. Some keep the name they use in the business world: Mrs. or Ms. Sarah Ode.

- Some women, when their children are grown, take back their maiden name and drop their former husband's surname altogether.

- Traditionally, a woman who has been married before does not have a formal engagement announcement in the newspaper, though some publications accept forthcoming marriage notices.

- Family and friends are informed of the news by letter or telephone.

- Traditionally, second-wedding ceremonies are small, with only close friends and family attending. Their invitations are telephoned or handwritten. The ceremony may be followed by a reception with many guests, or the festivities can be limited to close relatives and friends.

- For a large reception afterwards, the invitations should be printed or engraved and for a small one, handwritten notes suffice.

- The bride's parents may issue the invitations if the bride is young. A mature couple issues their own wedding invitations.

- The bride's home address is given so guests can respond. It is practical for a couple who have separate residences to enclose an "at home" card to indicate where they will be living after their marriage. They are small enough to fit comfortably in the invitation envelope along with other enclosures.

• If the bride is retaining the name that she has been using since her first marriage, or if she is assuming her maiden name, this is an excellent way of notifying everyone:

Ms. Jill Candace Ode
and
Mr. William Jones Westings
will be at home
after the first of July
11111 Permanent Drive
Baltimore, Maryland ZIP code

• The modern conservative divorced bride wears shades that lean to off-white and pale pastel hues in up-to-date lengths. Suits and silk dresses in the current style of the day are appropriate, and all aspects of her outfit follow the same mood. Head covering is optional or at the discretion of the house of worship.

The bridegroom's attire follows the formality of the bride's outfit, as does the attire of the attendants.

The bride might follow her attendant to the altar, or her mother, father, son, or a relative may escort her. The bridal couple might wish to walk together, hand in hand.

Traditionally, the bride has an honor attendant and the bridegroom has a best man.

If either member of the couple has children, he or she includes them in the wedding party.

The bridal couple have the same responsibilities to their attendants as they did for their first unions.

Formerly, bridal showers for second-time brides were unheard of. Today, intimate friends might host a shower.

Prewedding introduction parties, such as dinners, are wonderful ways of welcoming the couple. If time is too short before the wedding, feting the newlyweds is always fun.

Wedding cakes are always a part of any wedding reception.

Toasts and music are appropriate. Well-wishers are always welcome, and music enhances both the ceremony and the reception.

Mail marriage announcements, engraved or printed, as soon after the event as possible. Though they are not obligatory, they are an efficient way of communicating the couple's change of status to relatives, friends, acquaintances, and business associates who were *not invited to the wedding*.

The announcements note the bride's given name, maiden name, and married name:

If sent by her parents:

Mr. and Mrs. James Person Ode
have the honour of announcing
the marriage of their daughter
Jill Ode Hampenstance
to
Mr. William Jones Westings
Sunday, the first of January
One thousand nine hundred and ninety-five
in
Baltimore, Maryland

If sent by the couple:

Mrs. Frederick Eldon Hampenstance [traditional]
O R
Jill Ode Hampenstance
and
William Jones Westings
announce their marriage
[etc.]

The above is the same for a divorcée who wishes to announce her marriage and to use the name by which she is known:

Mrs. [or Ms.] Jill Ode Hampenstance [formal]
OR
Jill Ode Hampenstance
and
William Jones Westings
[etc.]

The announcement for a mature widow:

Mrs. Frederick Eldon Hampenstance
and
Mr. William Jones Westings
announce their marriage
[etc.]

A newspaper item is sent to the wedding desk at least ten days ahead of time for publication at the first available opportunity after the wedding. It can be as complete a story as wished, but the newspaper will edit to fit space restrictions. Some newspapers do not use the designations "Mr.," "Mrs.," or "Ms.," and do not be surprised if, within the story, references to either party are by surname only. Others insist on mentioning whether one or both have been married before, divorced, or widowed. There should be no objection to this, especially if there are children involved. Some people, however, do not wish to be reminded of the past and others feel it has nothing to do with what is happening now.

For release after January 1st:
Jill Ode Hampenstance and William Jones Westings were married in Baltimore, at the Calvert Hotel, in the presence of close family members, including the bride's children, Cynthia and

Joan Hampenstance, and the bridegroom's son, Jonathan Westings. The Rev. Holdings True was the officiating minister.

The bride, whose parents are Mr. and Mrs. James Person Ode
of Washington, D.C., is a financial consultant with Safe & Safe.
Westings is the son of Mr. and Mrs. Sanford Westings of Syra-
cuse, New York. He is vice president of the engineering consulting firm Engineering Design Corporation. Mr. and Mrs.
Westings' previous marriages ended in divorce. The couple resides in Baltimore.

Divorce

SENSITIVITY, INC.

Questions on divorce and remarriage are perennial. The trend
started in the sixties and has widened ever since. Wistfully, the
voice of the bride agrees with me that maybe hers is not such
an unusual situation—being divorced is commonplace. But for
one day in her life she would like to close her eyes and float
through the wedding day as if nothing had happened. Yes, even
though her parents have been divorced for years.

Divorce is a family affair that, however old they are, constantly touches the offspring—especially if there are bitter feelings on one side or both.

The difference between a holiday and a wedding is that
Thanksgiving can be spent with one parent and Christmas with
the other. But from the time of the engagement to the day
of the wedding, there are decisions to be made that involve
both the bride's and the bridegroom's families. All the bridal
couple wants is that both sets of parents attend and participate
according to custom.

If a divorced couple could cooperate to make events up to
and including the wedding day as happy as can be for their
child, this segment could just deal with questions such as who
sits where in church and who sponsors the wedding. But can

two people overcome their resentment long enough to support their child?

Sometimes the problems that surface do not come out of old hurts but of wedding protocol. The father of the bride may have remarried and would like his wife at his side; his former wife, the mother of his child, wants to take her "rightful" place in the proceedings.

How about this complication: Her former husband has sent word through their daughter that neither parent's name will appear on the wedding invitations. It reads:

> *The honour of*
> *your presence is requested*
> *at the marriage of*
> *Miss Jill Candace Ode*
> *and*
> *Mr. Frederick Eldon Hampenstance*

Mr. Ode told his daughter that since he is paying for the entire wedding his decision is firm. However, his daughter was to let him know his former wife's reaction. Mrs. Ex was angry because the wording on the invitation makes it seem as if the bride's parents are uninterested and that the bride is without a sponsor. That is true, I told her, but it seems that a rule is only as firm as those who are willing to abide by it.

What if your former husband's name is on the first line and hers below? Never, Mrs. Ex responded. Her daughter, whose father married his current wife seven years ago, said that she did not appreciate being caught between her parents. If he wants it that way, she told her mother, so be it—especially since he is footing the bill. Mrs. Ex made mention of her meager alimony and said that taking on the wedding expenses was out of the question.

How about a compromise? Suggest that he and his wife be

first sponsors on the top line with your name listed under-neath? Never! was her prompt reply.

On the surface it might seem that Mr. Ode, as master of the purse strings, could issue edicts from his exalted financial po-sition. I suspect his former wife is not the only problem. More than likely, he is having a problem with his current wife. It is sometimes difficult for the second wife to take a back seat when her husband's child marries. It is a part of his past she does not share. Besides, she more than likely objects to a joint invitation with only his and his former wife's names on it.

Mr. Ode also knows that his former wife would not agree to his wife's name on the invitations, so being a man used to taking command, he issues his decision—no one's name apart from the young couple's will appear. Since the bride is living on her own, the R.S.V.P.'s go to her home anyway.

I agree with Mr. Ex's decision. When the principals stand on their principles, the only thing to do is to say that this is the way it is.

Sensitivity—you better believe it! From the start of the en-gagement, how does one avoid the anxiety that is bound to arise, whether between divorced parents of the bridal couple or between the couple themselves?

One mother, remarried twenty years ago, told me that she drew up a list of what to anticipate during the planning of the wedding—apart from the practical services of caterers, et cetera.

- Whose names will head the newspaper, engagement, and marriage announcements? It might be she and her husband along with the bride's father, or, her father may be men-tioned within the item: daughter also of . . .
- Who expects to escort the bride? Her natural father or her stepfather who has nurtured her since she was two years old? Will it be her natural father who generally has the

honor as long as he has been a part of her life, and how will her stepfather feel about taking a lesser role in the ceremony?
- Who gives the bride in marriage?
- Who heads the receiving line?

There are many other questions that arise that concern anyone planning a wedding. Look up the subject in the index.

Sensitivity is not only shown by parents of the bride but also by stepparents. Many questions are from women who have the responsibility of planning their stepdaughters' weddings from beginning to end, taking extreme care not to appear as if they are usurping the brides' natural mothers.

WHEN BITTERNESS REIGNS

"BRIDE'S STEPMOTHER HOGS PHOTO SESSION" should be the headline at one wedding.

The father of the bride and his wife are paying for everything; the mother of the bride is lucky she is invited. During the picture taking, the photographer wanted to take one of the bride's mother with the bride and bridegroom in the center and the bride's father on the other side of them. The photographer had taken similar ones with the bridegroom's parents on either side of the bridal couple and others with the stepmother, the bridal couple, and the bride's father. Mrs. Stepmother insisted she be part of the photograph in which the bride's mother appeared. When the photographer tried to explain that the bride should have a shot with her natural parents, Mrs. Stepmother would not hear of it. After all, she reasoned aloud, it was her money that was paying for the service.

The bride's mother is still grieving over that one.

If you iz, then I ain't. But if you ain't, then I iz, goes the silly little ditty. She says to her children: If he brings his new wife then

I will not attend Thanksgiving dinner (your wedding, the baby's christening, or whatever the occasion may be).

Mrs. Newlywed, whose daughter was being married, wanted to know if she should include her husband in the wedding invitations or the newspaper announcement, since they had only been married for a year and a half.

Do you think he will be hurt if you do not include him? I inquired. Not at all, was the response. On the contrary, he refuses to attend her daughter's wedding because he did not want to see her ex-husband. Everyone, including the bride, urges him to attend but he is adamant.

Finally, the reason surfaced. His son, whose wedding was to take place within two months, told his father not to bring his wife because his mother—who remains unmarried—is refusing to attend any function if he comes with that woman.

Ladies and Gentlemen, that is a classical piece of manipulation. This is a way some people have learned to operate. Instead of coming directly to the point with his second wife about the problem that his son was having with his mother, the stepfather chose a roundabout way of solving a dilemma.

PENDING DIVORCE

Q: *My only daughter is being married and I am determined she'll have an elegant formal wedding. However, my wife and I are in the midst of a divorce. It may be final by the time the wedding invitations are mailed. However, suppose it is not? I am in a quandary as to how to word the invitation.*

Since you cannot be sure of the timing of your divorce or of the complications that might suddenly develop, I suggest:

The parents of
Miss Jill Candace Ode

> request the honour of your presence
> at her marriage
> to
> Mr. Frederick Eldon Hampenstance
> O R
> The honour of your presence
> is requested
> at the marriage of
> Miss Jill Candace Ode
> to
> Mr. Frederick Eldon Hampenstance
> [etc.]

Under ideal circumstances, divorced parents can issue a joint invitation. It is customary for the mother's name to appear first:

> Mrs. Sarah Manning Ode
> O R
> Mrs. Sarah Ode
> and
> Mr. James Person Ode
> request the honour of your presence
> at the marriage of their daughter
> [etc.]

If both parents have remarried and are sharing the expenses, then the invitation can be a joint one:

> Mr. and Mrs. George Steadfast
> and
> Mr. and Mrs. James Person Ode
> request the honour of your presence
> at the marriage of
> Miss Jill Candace Ode
> to
> Mr. Frederick Eldon Hampenstance
> [etc.]

Should only the bride's divorced mother issue the invitation:

> *Mrs. Sarah Manning Ode*
> *requests the honour of your presence*
> *at the marriage of her daughter*
> *[etc.]*

Q: I've dreamed of the day my parents would escort me down the aisle and stand with me under the canopy for the traditional Jewish wedding ceremony. My fiancé wants his parents to do the same, but I feel it would be awkward. His parents have been divorced for the last ten years, and his father has remarried. When I phoned his mother, who lives in another state, I detected resentment. Will it look all right if I walk with my parents and he doesn't?

Your fiancé should tell his parents how much it means to him if they would walk with him. They may surprise him and acquiesce—after all, enough time has elapsed since the divorce for the healing process to have taken place.

After you and your parents are under the canopy, the bridegroom's mother walks from the first row to stand under the canopy to the right of the best man and his father on his son's left.

That much the couple should do for their son.

If he receives a negative answer, he should discuss it with his rabbi. If no one budges, the bridegroom could walk down the aisle, or come from the side of the synagogue, with his best man.

GETTING-EVEN TIME?

People call a newspaper asking all types of questions. What time is it in Timbuktu? I have an appointment in Samarra, shall I take an umbrella? What shall I do? My cat is caught in the mousetrap. So you can imagine the sorts of questions that came to the Bridal Desk, both from those who merely wish to know the correct order of things and from those who have serious problems.

There are times when I can clearly see that what the inquirer really wants to know is how to use an important occasion to get even. It has nothing to do with the celebration, the people hosting the event, those being honored, or those invited. This is done without regard for the innocent. Some people live by the adage "Don't get mad, get even," and if others are hurt because they happen to be there, then so be it.

Vindictiveness sometimes waits years to pounce. It looks for a time when it really counts, when it really hurts. Some use a wedding, an anniversary, even a funeral.

Q: *My father, who has remarried, and my mother had been separated for a few years before their divorce five years ago. He is paying for the food at the reception and the wedding cake. Mother simply cannot afford to contribute because she's always suing for back alimony payments. My fiancé and I are paying for everything else: church, liquor, photographs, music, and all the sundry items.*

The receiving line is going to be in the church right after the ceremony. Father says that since he is paying for the wedding reception, he has the right to insist that he and his wife, and not my mother, sit in the first pew, and that she also shouldn't be in the receiving line. I'm not sure how to handle the situation.

There are wedding books in the library with guidelines on dealing with divorced parents. Approach your father by asking him to read what the wedding books advise. He may see how awkward his demands are.

Your mother is seated last and that signals to everyone that the ceremony is to begin. Your father and his wife sit in the third pew.

For your father to insist otherwise puts him and his wife in a bad light. He creates the same impression by objecting to your mother rightfully heading the receiving line. He should remember that at the reception your mother will be an honored guest.

DIVORCED TILL DEATH DO US PART

Ladies and Gentlemen, the first rule to remember is that the bride's natural parents play special roles in the marrying of their child. Their union might be dissolved but the issue from that marriage is not divorced from either parent. For one side to try to exclude the other is cruel.

I do not know the young lady's father, so she must decide whether he will withhold the support he has offered if she insists on objecting to the stand he is taking. I do not know if her nature is such that she can take a strong position, or whether it is even feasible at this time. It depends on the caterers and other services, who hold deposits, if she can change her plans to fit her pocketbook.

As I have said many times before: advice is only as good as the receiver's ability to take it, and, what is more, only that person knows the full story.

Ladies and Gentlemen, after a certain amount of time has passed after the breakup, most divorced couples, whether remarried or not, are able to come together at functions to celebrate family occasions. They participate freely and without trepidation and do not feel a sense of estrangement at the wedding.

Gracious stepmothers and even-tempered divorced parents do not titillate our sense of curiosity. A famous media anchorperson made the observation that very few good deeds make the headlines in newspapers. I have used other people's unhappy experiences hoping to help those in similar positions.

Among my friends are three married couples—three mature men and three mature women. They met at a singles' group when all but one, who was a widower, had recently separated or were in the throes of divorce. All six have children from their first marriages.

Each couple was married in the presence of their immediate families in simple ceremonies—one couple by a judge, the other two by justices of the peace at a courthouse. All had small, intimate receptions given by close friends.

The women had become good friends and nurtured one another through the different problems of divorce. Afterwards, when one by one they met the men they married, they learned from one another's experiences how to handle the adjustment period not only with their new husbands, but with stepchildren.

The mingling of stepchildren led to the displacing of the youngest child who was not the youngest any longer, an only child who was unused to sharing, and jealous moments and resentments. It took time, understanding, and effort. Most importantly, each couple worked in unison by not allowing their children to manipulate them.

To me, they are role models for building the step-by-step process of harmonious relationships. We do not leave this world unscathed, but if you have a good support group you are fortunate indeed.

. . . And so, Ladies and Gentlemen, the questions keep coming in that are never quite the same as before, though the subject might be. Some are surprisingly different. It is an interesting world.

Index

277